THE RAPTURE
THE REMNANT
AND THE RETURN

A Deeper Look into Christ's Second Coming

SEAN EASTHAM

Cloudbound
PUBLISHERS

Unless otherwise indicated, all Scripture quotations are from The Holy Bible, New King James Version. Copyright © 1982 by Thomas Nelson, Inc. Used by permission. All rights reserved.

Verses marked NIV are taken from The Holy Bible, New International Version. Copyright 1973, 1978, 1984, 2011 by Biblica, Inc. Used by permission. All rights reserved worldwide.

All emphasis in Scripture quotations is added by the author.

Backcover photo by Sean Eastham
Cover concept by Sean Eastham
Cover design by Kathryn E. Campbell

The Rapture, The Remnant, and The Return
Copyright © 2014 by Sean Eastham
All rights reserved.

Published by Cloudbound Publishers
Astoria, Oregon 97103
cloudboundpublishers@gmail.com

Print Edition ISBN 978-0-9960906-0-5
EPUB Edition ISBN 978-0-9960906-1-2
MOBI Edition ISBN 978-0-9960906-2-9

Printed in the United States of America

To Grandma Josie

Thank you for your life long service to our Lord.

Your reward will truly be great.

Contents

How to Use This Book 6
Foreword 8

Part One | 1948
The Year That Opened the Door to Bible Prophecy 11
Section 1 13
Section 2 15
Section 3 16
Section 4 18
Section 5 20
Section 6 21
Section 7 23
Section 8 25
Section 9 26
Section 10 27
Section 11 28
Section 12 30

Part Two | Eighty Years?
The Generation That Will Not Pass Away 33
Section 1 35
Section 2 38
Section 3 41
Section 4 43
Section 5 45
Section 6 47
Section 7 51

Part Three | Imminency
Understanding the Timing of the Rapture 55
Section 1 57
Section 2 61
Section 3 65

Section 4 67
Section 5 70
Section 6 73
Section 7 76
Section 8 83
Section 9 85
Section 10 89
Section 11 92
Section 12 94
Section 13 97

Part Four | Where Have They Gone?
An Explanation for Those Not Taken When the People Vanished ... 101
Section 1 103
Section 2 106
Section 3 111
Section 4 114
Section 5 117
Section 6 122
Section 7 125
Section 8 127
Section 9 129
Section 10 134
Section 11 136
Section 12 138
Section 13 141
Section 14 145
Section 15 147
Section 16 152
Section 17 154
Section 18 156
Section 19 158
Appendix 161

How to Use This Book

This book is written as an appeal for believers in Christ, and anyone with an ear to hear the Word of God, to wake up to the reality that Jesus Christ is coming soon for His Church. Judgment is about to be unleashed upon the world for its sin. The author will show evidence through Scripture, as well as events in modern history, to convince and persuade you to open your eyes to Bible prophecy and get excited and right with God. Jesus Christ is about to act in a big way on planet earth! You must be prepared spiritually for what is about to happen. Be assured that your confidence can only lie in one place in these uncertain days we are living in. How you live your life today and what you believe will have eternal consequences and or rewards. There are no blurred lines in God's Word. Believe in the truth of the Bible, and you will be prepared for eternity and God's plans for humanity.

Unlike most chapter books, this book is written in the format of parts and sections for ease of reading, study, and reference. This is not light reading material. Many of the ideas and subject matter expressed require deep thought and contemplation. Reading this book several times may be needed to fully grasp the magnitude and timeliness of its content. A suggestion would be to devote at least twenty to forty minutes of uninterrupted reading and study in a quiet place. Reading one part or sections of one part in one sitting may be beneficial. Taking notes, or jotting down any thoughts or scriptures may be helpful as you read.

Part four of this book—"Where have they gone?" is unique in that it presents the gospel and provides an explanation for those who have missed the Rapture. It can be a guide to assist those left behind who are seeking God. This will help them understand what has happened and what to expect in their near future according to Bible prophecy. The ultimate hope of part four is to bring unbelievers to a saving knowledge of the Lord Jesus Christ. It is informative and helpful no matter what point in God's future timeline you are reading it.

An idea of how to use part four as a future gospel tool, would be to leave a copy of the book or just part four on your kitchen counter, coffee table, or anywhere someone would easily find it in your home. Write on it in big red letters, "Read Me." After you have been raptured, unsaved friends, family, and co-workers will likely be going to your home to check up on you. Finding a copy could be just what the Holy Spirit may use to help save their soul at that time.

Finally, please feel free to distribute this book to anyone and everyone you feel led to give it to. If you have an electronic version, download it, e-mail it, or spread through social media. You may also leave a printed copy lying around for someone to grab. Spread the word. The message must be heard. People need to know what Jesus Christ is about to do and the provision He has made to save them. The world is running out of time! God bless you and thank you for your part in spreading a message that must be heard.

Foreword

In 2004, the author's grandmother wrote in her journal what she felt the Lord was speaking to her heart that particular day. The message, used in this book for illustrative purposes, is scripturally sound with biblical truths prophetic in nature. The message is not an excerpt from The Bible, nor is it to be thought of as an addition to The Bible.

November 15, 2004

My God, who and what are you?

I have said in My Word, I have declared Myself to be the "I AM." Everything, everyone revolves around "Me." Whether your face is toward Me, or your back turned from Me, no one can remove himself.

It is like the sun with the planets revolving around it. Not one can say, "I'm not a part of the pull." You will never experience any place, or time where "I AM" is not. This is the reason the lost will grind their teeth and weep and wail. Awareness without hope is utter despair.

All over the earth I am calling……calling……Oh turn around and come to Me. The price has been paid. A way has been prepared for you by God the Son.

Oh the cunning deception of the evil one and the foolishness of mankind's unacceptance of this message, which seal them to eternal doom.

Hear Me when I say……I am the way, the truth, and the life. No one comes to the Father and the new beginnings He has for them, now and for eternity, except through Me.

*See, the Lord is coming with fire,
and his chariots are like a whirlwind;
he will bring down his anger with fury,
and his rebuke with flames of fire.
For with fire and with his sword
the Lord will execute judgment on all people,
and many will be those slain by the Lord.*

—Isaiah 66:15-16 NIV

*And He has on His robe and
on His thigh a name written:*
KING OF KING AND LORD OF LORDS.

—Revelation 19:16

*Because you have kept My command to persevere,
I will also keep you from the hour of trial
which shall come upon the whole world,
to test those who dwell on the earth.*

—Revelation 3:10

Part One

1948

The Year That Opened the Door to Bible Prophecy

Section 1

According to biblical prophecies over 2500 years ago, in the last days God will draw together His chosen people from the four corners of the world and reunite them in their own land—the land promised to their forefathers, and they would prosper. Since the year 721 B.C., there had not been a nation on the planet called "Israel" until May 14, 1948. This day in history marks the most significant prophetic event in the Bible to be fulfilled since the first century. This day started the clock and has since launched into effect scores of other prophecies that could not take place until this nation once again existed. Israel came back to life and something profound happened across the globe. It changed the world forever! This event has created the most exciting and anticipated time to be a Christian since the days Jesus Christ walked the earth!

Since Israel's rebirth, the days we are now living in are referred to in Scripture as "the last days." This is a time that is doomed with unthinkable terror, war, and destruction. During this time God will judge His chosen nation—Israel, and all on the planet who have rejected Christ as the Savior of their souls. These days will see the fall of America as the world's super power and will see the rise of a new world leader, who will unite most of the world into a one world government, one world economy, and one world religion. This leader, known in the Bible as the Antichrist, a man empowered by Satan[1] himself, will ultimately unfold other prophesies such as a seven year peace treaty[2] with Israel that will begin what Scripture calls, "the time of Jacob's trouble"[3] or the Tribulation[4]. This will be a seven year period of God's judgment on the earth[5] that is so catastrophic, if God himself did not put an end to it, the Bible says that *"no flesh would be saved."*[6]

The good news is that prior to the Tribulation and revealing of the Antichrist[7], Christ will rescue and remove His followers from the world in the Rapture[8]. He will return at the end of the Tribulation with His saints[9] and put an end to evil on the earth. His return will usher in an era where Christ will physically rule the planet as King and establish His earthly kingdom of peace and justice for 1000 years, the time known as the "Millennium" referred to in the book of Revelation[10]. At His return, He will welcome those into His new kingdom who serve Him as Lord, and will cast all those who have rejected Him into outer darkness. After His millennial reign, God will then purify the earth with fire[11] and create a new planet earth and a new universe not under the curse of sin[12]. He will bring His heavenly city, the "New Jerusalem," down to this new earth[13] where He will rule and reign with His saints and creation for all eternity.

Since Christ left us nearly 2000 years ago and went back to heaven, His Church has been waiting for His return and these events to transpire. Scripture makes it clear that none of these end times prophesies would begin to be fulfilled until what occurred on May 14, 1948, the re-establishment and rebirth of the nation Israel.

In the year 1948, other events took place in the world that began to set the groundwork and create a global mindset for the rise of a leader, who could unite the world in deception. The Bible states that in the last days knowledge will increase. Technologies have now risen that will assist the Antichrist in controlling a one world government, economy, and religion, such as the invention of computers, a unified banking system, and increased travel and communication. People's hearts will and have become hardened and they will be easily deceived. As times get worse, things like disasters, catastrophes, wars, corruption, crime, and strife will increase in frequency and magnitude, such as a woman's labor in child birth increases in intensity. Look at the events of 1948 and see for yourself that 1948 was the prophetic year that started the clock and the countdown for the end of this age as we know it.

Part One—Section 2

Re-establishment of the Nation Israel

Ezekiel 36:24,28 (570 B.C.) 24 For I will take you from among the nations, gather you out of all countries, and bring you into your own land. 28 Then you shall dwell in the land that I gave to your fathers; you shall be My people, and I will be your God.

Isaiah 11:11,12 (700 B.C.) 11 It shall come to pass in that day that the Lord shall set His hand again the second time to recover the remnant of His people who are left... 12 He will set up a banner for the nations, and will assemble the outcasts of Israel, and gather together the dispersed of Judah from the four corners of the earth.

- *May 14, 1948*—David Ben-Gurion proclaimed the establishment of the State of Israel. On that day, Ben-Gurion began the role of prime minister, which he served until 1954.

- *May 14, 1948*—President Truman recognizes Israel as a sovereign nation.

- *May 14, 1948*—Arab-Israeli War begins. Israel was attacked by the countries of Lebanon, Syria, Iraq, Egypt, and Saudi Arabia in an unsuccessful attempt to destroy the new nation and prevent its formation.

Part One—Section 3
One World Government

Revelation 13:7,8 7 And authority was given him over every tribe, tongue, and nation. 8 All who dwell on the earth will worship him... (Referencing the Antichrist)

- *1946*—Winston Churchill calls for a "United States of Europe."

- *April 7, 1948*—World Health Organization founded by the United Nations.

- *April 30, 1948*—Organization of American States (OAS) founded. It is a regional international organization consisting of 35 independent states of the Americas headquartered in Washington D.C.

- *April 1948*—The OAS adopts the (American Declaration of the Rights and Duties of Man), the world's first general human rights instrument.

- *June 24, 1948*—First World Health Assembly in Geneva.

- *September 14, 1948*—Ground breaking ceremony for the U.N. building.

- *October 5, 1948*—International Union for Conservation of Nature (IUCN) founded, (world's first global environmental organization).

- *December 12, 1948*—United Nations adopts the "Universal Declaration of Human Rights." It empowers the U.N. with authority to govern all nations.

- *1948*—The United Nations had 66 member nations. It added 128 more countries in 1949.

- *1949*—Council of Europe, the first pan-European organization founded. This organization led to the development of the European Union.

- *April 4, 1949*—North Atlantic Treaty Organization (NATO) founded. It was created to provide a collaborative measure of security against the rising Soviet Union. Initial members included the United States, Canada, United Kingdom, Denmark, Belgium, France, Iceland, Italy, Luxemburg, the Netherlands, Norway, and Portugal.

Part One—Section 4

One World Economy

Revelation 13:16,17 16 He causes all, both small and great, rich and poor, free and slave, to receive a mark on their right hand or on their foreheads, 17 and that no one may buy or sell except one who has the mark or the name of the beast, or the number of his name.

- *Quote from Paul-Henry Spaak*—Spaak was the first president of the United Nations General Assembly and served in that role from 1946 to 1957. In 1957 Spaak stated,

"We do not want another committee, we have too many already. What we want is a man of sufficient stature to hold the allegiance of all the people and to lift us up out of the economic morass into which we are sinking. Send us such a man, and whether he be God or devil, we will receive him." —Paul-Henry Spaak

- *1944*—The World Bank is founded.

- *July 27, 1944*—International Monetary Fund (IMF) founded.

- *January 1, 1948*—General Agreement on Tariffs and Trade (GATT) founded. GATT changed in 1995 to be known as the World Trade Organization (WTO).

- *March 17, 1948*—Treaty of Brussels is signed, (Military, Economic, Social, and Cultural collaboration of the countries of Belgium, France, U.K., Netherlands, and Luxembourg).

- *April 3, 1948*—President Truman signs the Marshall Plan, ($5 billion in aid to 16 countries) also known as the Economic Cooperation Act (ECA).

- *April 16, 1948*—Organization for Economic Cooperation and Development (OEEC) founded.
- *July 5, 1948*—National Health Service begins Universal Health Care in the United Kingdom.
- *1948*—The World Trade Organization states that since 1948 world trade has consistently grown faster than world output.

Part One—Section 5
One World Religion

Revelation 13:12,13 12 And he exercises all authority of the first beast in his presence, and causes the earth and those who dwell in it to worship the first beast... 13 He performs great signs, so that he even makes fire come down from heaven on the earth in the sight of men.

- *March 8, 1948*—McColkum vs. Board of Education, (U.S. Supreme Court rules that religious instruction in public schools violates the U.S. Constitution).

- *April 1948*—Scientist publish the Alpher-Bethe-Gamon paper, (physicists' explanation of the Big Bang Theory).

- *August 23, 1948*—World Council of Churches (WCC) founded. They held their first assembly in Amsterdam.

- *1948*—Decline of Christianity in America. The Gallup poll began tracking religious identification in 1948. In 1948 ninety-one percent of Americans claimed to be Christian. In 2008 only seventy-seven percent said they were Christian. In 1948 two percent claimed to be atheist, which rose to twelve percent in 2008.

- *1993*—International Religious Initiative (URI) founded. (72 nation members as of 2009. Modeled after the U.N., it promotes inter-faith cooperation to create social change).

Part One—Section 6
Increase in Knowledge

Daniel 12:4 "But you, Daniel, shut up the words, and seal the book until the time of the end; many shall run to and fro, and knowledge shall increase."

- *June 21, 1948*—Creation of the first prototype of a RAM stored program computer.

- *June 30, 1948*—Bell Labs introduces the transistor chip, (first bi-polar junction transistor). This changed the course of history for computers and electronics.

- *1948*—IBM produces the first programmable vacuum tube-based calculator.

- *1948*—Development and sale of the Polaroid camera.

- *1948*—Cybernetics book published by Norman Wiener. (Cybernetics is the science of creating a living machine).

- *1948*—Holographic Imagery, (the science of producing three dimensional pictures) is created by Dennis Gabor. In 1971 he received the Noble Prize for physics for this invention.

- *1948*—Invention of light sensitive electro-mechanical robots, a precursor of modern robots.

- *1948*—Operation begins in Detroit of the first transfer machines used in manufacturing engine blocks. They performed 550 tooling operations in 15 minutes, greatly increasing the production of engines.

- *1948*—August Piccard constructs his first bathyscaphe, an underwater vessel designed for deep ocean exploration.

- *1948*—Development of the X-ray reflection microscope for the examination of living cells. Its use was in the areas of medicine and astronomy. It was later used to take X-ray photographs of distant galaxies.

Part One—Section 7

Nation against Nation

Matthew 24:7 For nation will rise against nation, and kingdom against kingdom…

- *1947*—Doomsday Clock established, (Countdown to global destruction). Set at 11:53 p.m. in 1947 for threat of world nuclear destruction. It has been reset throughout the years based on world events. It was last set at 11:55 p.m. on January 14, 2014.

- *1947*—Pakistan gains independence from India.

- *January 4, 1948*—Burma gains independence from United Kingdom.

- *February 4, 1948*—Sri Lanka gains independence from United Kingdom.

- *November 30, 1947 to May 14, 1948*—Civil war in Mandatory Palestine.

- *April 9, 1948*—Deir Yassin Massacre, (107 villagers died).

- *April 13, 1948*—Hadassah Medical Convoy Massacre, (79 dead).

- *April 1948*—Apartheid established in South Africa.

- *May 14, 1948*—Arab–Israeli War begins.

- *June 24, 1948*—Cold War, (Berlin blockade begins). The Berlin airlift began three days prior.

- *August 15, 1948*—South Korean uprising, (Established Republic of Korea, South Korea).

- *September 9, 1948*—North Korea established, (Democratic People's Republic of Korea).

- *November 16, 1948*—Operation Magic Carpet, (transporting Jews from Yemen to Israel).

- *December 28, 1948*—Muslim Brotherhood assassinates Egyptian Prime Minister.

- *1949*—Peoples Republic of China established.

Part One—Section 8
Disasters and Catastrophes

Luke 21:11 And there will be great earthquakes in various places, and famines, and pestilences; and there will be fearful sights and great signs from heaven.

- *March 16, 1948*—Largest flood in the history of Brampton, Ontario, (2000 homes damaged or destroyed).

- *May 25, 1948*—Litang earthquake in Litang, China, (7.2 Richter, more than 800 deaths, 600 homes destroyed.)

- *May 30, 1948*—Columbia River dike breaks destroying Vanport, OR. (Kills 15, thousands homeless).

- *June 16, 1948*—DC-6 airline crashes in Pennsylvania, (Kills 43).

- *June 28, 1948*—Fuji earthquake in Fukui, Japan, (7.3 Richter, kills 5390, injures 22,000, destroys 39,000 homes).

- *July 28, 1948*—200 killed in a chemical plant explosion in Germany.

- *October 6, 1948*—Ashgabat earthquake in Soviet Union, (7.3 Richter, up to 176,000 dead, 12th deadliest quake of all time). Possible cause of the quake was the Soviets first atomic bomb test.

- *October 27, 1948*—Donora smog disaster, (Donora, Pennsylvania). One of the worst air pollution disasters in U.S. history. Smog from a steel plant killed 20 humans, 800 animals, and sickened 7000 people, half the town's population.

- *1948*—A pack of wolves kill 40 children in Russia.

- *1948*—9 out of 10 largest recorded earthquakes in history have occurred since 1948.

Part One—Section 9

Corruption, Crime, and Strife

2 Timothy 3:1-5 But know this, that in the last days perilous times will come: for men will be lovers of themselves, lovers of money, boasters, proud, blasphemers, disobedient to parents, unthankful, unholy, unloving, unforgiving, slanderers, without self-control, brutal, despisers of good, traitors, headstrong, haughty, lovers of pleasure rather than lovers of God, having a form of godliness but denying its power. And from such people turn away!

- *January 26, 1948*—Teigin Poison Case, (A man pretends to be a doctor, poisons 12 bank employees and then steals the money).
- *January 30, 1948*—Mahatma Gandhi is assassinated.
- *March 1948*—Hell's Angels are founded.
- *April 1948*—Jehu Uprising, (Residents revolt on Jehu Island, South Korea, resulting in up to 30,000 deaths).
- *April 9, 1948*—Assassination of Jorge Eliecer Gaitan, (Starts riots in Bogotá that begin 10 years of violence in all of Columbia).
- *June 16, 1948*—First commercial airline high jacking, (Plane crashes, 26 dead).
- *December 9, 1948*—Convention on the Prevention and Punishment of the Crime of Genocide. It was one of the first United Nation conventions regarding humanitarian issues. The convention provided a definition for the crime of genocide.

Part One—Section 10
Signs in the Stars

Luke 21:25,26 25 "And there will be signs in the sun, in the moon, and in the stars; and on the earth distress of nations, with perplexity, the sea and the waves roaring; 26 men's hearts failing them from fear and the expectation of those things which are coming on the earth, for the powers of the heavens will be shaken."

- *January 1948*— USAF pilot is killed chasing a U.F.O.

- *February 16, 1948*—Miranda, innermost moon of Uranus discovered.

- *June 3, 1948*—Palomar Observatory Telescope is finished in California.

- *June 11, 1948*—First monkey astronaut (Albert 1) launched into space.

- *July 1948*—DC-3 airliner over Montgomery, AL spots a U.F.O.

- *1948*—Completion of the Schmidt Telescope, (Largest in the world).

- *1949-1950*—Blood moon tetrad, (Four consecutive lunar eclipses coinciding with Jewish feast days). April 13, 1949—Passover, October 7, 1949—Feast of Tabernacles, April 2, 1950—Passover, September 26, 1950—Feast of Tabernacles

Part One—Section 11

It is clear that something prophetically profound occurred in 1948. This is an examination of just one year in history, but this year has been like none other before or since. The blue print for the end times, or the "signs of the times" was drafted in days of old. God's chosen nation, once again united, catapults prophetic Scripture into play and the drama has since unfolded and exploded exponentially up to the day we are now in. What was once a glimmer of a future time, has now become an everyday reality that most turn a blind eye to, or are completely ignorant of, including many who profess Christ. The Bible reveals that final prophecies would not come to pass and Christ would not return in judgment until the people of Israel were back in their land. It happened. Israel came back and Bible prophecy came to life!

The Bible states that one day the Lord will give a reward—the crown of righteousness, to those who love His appearing, who are earnestly awaiting and actively seeking His imminent return. The days we are living in is not the time to be overwhelmed with the "cares of this world," but rather a time to be filling our lamps with oil and trimming our wicks. As Jesus explained in the parable of the ten virgins[14], five were ready and waiting when the bridegroom arrived—had their lamps filled with oil, their wicks trimmed, and were prepared to leave at a moment's notice. The five foolish virgins were lazy and unconcerned with what they knew would someday happen. It was too late for them when the signs of the bridegroom appeared. They were unprepared to leave and were not accepted, or found worthy to be called a bride.

Jesus in His own words made it very clear when He said:

Luke 21:34-36 34 "But take heed to yourselves, lest your hearts be weighed down with carousing, drunkenness, and cares of this life, and that Day come on you unexpectedly. 35 For it will come as a snare on all those who dwell on the face of the whole earth.

36 Watch therefore, and pray always that you may be counted worthy to escape all these things that will come to pass, and to stand before the Son of Man."

Luke 21:28 *Now when these things begin to happen, look up and lift your heads, because your redemption draws near.*

Part One—Section 12
World Wide Earthquake History

Jesus taught that in the last days just before He returned there would be obvious signs that the time was near. One of those signs that He spoke of would be an increase in *"great earthquakes"* and tsunamis. He prophesied that these events would increase in frequency and magnitude. He compared it to a woman going through child birth. The birth pains become more frequent and more intense just before delivery.

With today's technology, monitoring earthquakes has come down to a science. It has become one of the most obvious "last day" signs to monitor and track, proving that Bible prophecy is being fulfilled and the return of the Lord is near. In looking at modern earthquake data, there is no doubt that what the Lord spoke of is coming true, especially since 1948.

> Jesus said, *Luke 21:11,25,26 11 And there will be great earthquakes in various places...25...and on the earth distress of nations, with perplexity, the sea and the waves roaring; 26 men's hearts failing them from fear and the expectation of those things which are coming on the earth, for the powers of the heavens will be shaken.*

Increase in Earthquake Frequency

Recorded quakes with a magnitude 6.0 and greater

- From 1900 to 1939 there were 12 quakes.
- From 1940 to 1949 there were 51.
- From 1950 to 1959 there were 475.
- From 1960 to 1969 there were 1056.
- From 1970 to 1979 there were 1184.
- From 1980 to 1989 there were 1085.
- From 1990 to 1999 there were 1525.
- From 2000 to 2012 there were 2092.

Increase in Earthquake Magnitude

Ten Largest Recorded Earthquakes

Date	Location	Magnitude
1. May 22, 1960	Valdivia, Chile	9.5
2. March 28, 1964	Prince William Sound, Alaska	9.2
3. December 26, 2004	Sumatra, Indonesia	9.1
4. March 11, 2011	Sendai, Japan	9.0
5. November 4, 1952	Kamchatka, Russia	9.0
6. February 27, 2010	Bio-Bio, Chile	8.8
7. January 31, 1906	Ecuador	8.8
8. February 4, 1965	Aleutian Islands	8.7
9. March 28, 2005	Northern Sumatra, Indonesia	8.6
10. August 15, 1950	Assam, Tibet	8.6

Increase in Earthquake Death Toll

Ten Deadliest Earthquakes Since 1900

Date	Location	Magnitude	Death Toll
1. January 12, 2010	Haiti	7.0	316,000
2. July 27, 1976	Tangshan, China	7.5	242,769
3. December 26, 2004	Sumatra, Indonesia	9.1	227,898
4. December 16, 1920	Haiyuan, China	7.8	200,000
5. September 1, 1923	Kanto, Japan	7.9	142,800
6. October 6, 1948	Ashgabat, Turkmenistan	7.3	110,000
7. May 12, 2008	Eastern Sichuan, China	7.9	87, 587
8. October 8, 2005	Pakistan	7.6	86,000
9. December 28, 1908	Messina, Italy	7.2	72,000
10. May 31, 1970	Chimbote, Peru	7.9	70,000

Data Source: USGS, Japan Meteorological Agency, Wikipedia

Part One—Scripture References

1) Revelation 13:4, 2 Thessalonians 2:9
2) Daniel 9:27
3) Jeremiah 30:7
4) Revelation 7:14, Matthew 24:21
5) Daniel 12:1
6) Matthew 24:22
7) 2 Thessalonians 2:3-4, Revelation 13:1-8
8) 1 Thessalonians 4:13-18, I Corinthians 15:51-54, Luke 21:34-36
9) Revelation 19:14, 1 Thessalonians 3:13
10) Revelation 20
11) 2 Peter 3:7,10
12) Revelation 21:1, Isaiah 65:17 and 66:22 and 51:6
13) Revelation 21:2
14) Matthew 25:1-13

Part Two

Eighty Years?

The Generation That Will Not Pass Away

Section 1

The Bible speaks of a time and a future generation that will see all the events transpire that have been prophesied in the Bible regarding these "last days." From the first signs, to coming of the Lord Jesus Christ in great power, glory, and judgment, a remnant of this generation will be here to witness the fulfillment of Scripture as the Lord Jesus establishes His earthly millennial reign. For centuries, Bible scholars have been trying to interpret and understand the mystery surrounding this debated generation. They have asked questions such as: "When will this generation begin? How long is a generation? And what is a generation?"

Based on clues left behind in the Scriptures, people throughout history have tried to pinpoint when our Lord would return. The Bible clearly teaches to watch out for people trying to declare the day of His return, so that you're not deceived. The Bible says that no one can know the day or hour of the Lord's return. Though we will not know the exact day or hour, Jesus made it clear that if this generation is watching, paying attention to the signs, following the Lord and walking in His ways, they would understand the season and recognize the signs of the times. Ultimately, they should be lifting their eyes to the skies waiting for that "blessed hope" of escape known as the "Rapture," or the "Resurrection" of the saints.

One day Jesus had a conversation with His disciples on the Mount of Olives. This conversation has come to be known as the "Olivet Discourse," and is found in the chapters of *Matthew 24, Mark 13*, and *Luke 21*. Before going onto the mountain, Jesus had told His disciples as they walked near the temple, that the entire temple and everything around it would one day be destroyed. Not one stone of the temple would be left upon another. This idea perplexed His followers. They came back to Him with a couple questions.

On the Mount of Olives they asked Him, *"Tell us, when will these things be? And what will be the sign of Your coming, and the end of the age?"*

(Matthew 24:3) Jesus answered in great detail as He prophesied two distinct events. He went on to reveal what would happen surrounding the time the temple would be destroyed, as well as what the signs of the times will look like when He returns to earth in glory. As we know from history, the temple in Jerusalem was destroyed in 70 A.D. by the Romans and their tyrannical ruler Titus. At that time, the Christians and Jews were persecuted, killed, and scattered across the world. You can see from reading the Olivet Discourse that prophecy was fulfilled as told by Jesus. You can also see Christ's description of His return and the condition of the world during that time. Some of the most precise revelations in Scripture about Christ's return and the last days are found in this discussion with His disciples.

Jesus went on to explain that in the last days before His return there would be false Christs, wars, nations and kingdoms fighting with each other, famines, pestilences, and great earthquakes in various places. He said this would be the beginning of sorrows. Jesus said further that those who loved Him would be hated, and that hate and betrayal will be common. There would be false prophets deceiving many, and lawlessness will rule the day. People's hearts would be hardened, but His gospel will be preached in all the world and to all the nations.

Jesus told them there would be a time of great tribulation more severe than at any time since the beginning of the world, or ever would be. So devastating will this time be, that all flesh would be destroyed unless He put that time to an end, but for the sake of His people He will end that time with His glorious return. (Here Jesus is talking about the seven year Tribulation period under the rule of the Antichrist, written by the prophet Daniel—also known as the 70th week of Daniel.)

Jesus then described what that day will be like when He returns. He said immediately after those days of great tribulation the sun and moon would be darkened, stars would fall from heaven, and the powers of the heavens will be shaken. He said He would then appear, and all the tribes of the earth will mourn as they see Him coming on the clouds of heaven with great power and glory. His angels, with the sound of a great trumpet, will gather together His elect from the four winds, from one end of heaven to the other. His enemies will then be utterly destroyed and thus will begin His magnificent earthly reign.

What a glorious and dreadful Day this will be. These signs and events are not to be confused with the Rapture of the Church. There are no signs mentioned in Scripture to indicate when the Rapture will occur. These events are specific to the time of the Tribulation and the Lord's glorious return at the end of those days in fulfilling His promise to be the King of His chosen people. What can be said of the Rapture is that the generation that sees these signs of the Lord's return can know for certain that their escape from this judgment is soon on the horizon. We are instructed to be ready and look to the skies, for our redemption is drawing near. What a glorious Day this will be.

Jesus then told his disciples a parable known as the "Parable of the Fig Tree." From this parable, we learn of the generation that will not pass away, that will see these signs, and His glorious return. As quoted from *Matthew 24:32-35*:

> 32 *"Now learn this parable from the fig tree: When its branch has already become tender and puts forth leaves, you know that summer is near. 33 So you also, when you see all these things, know that it is near—at the doors! 34 Assuredly, I say to you, this generation will by no means pass away till all these things take place. 35 Heaven and earth will pass away, but My words will by no means pass away."*

What did Jesus mean when He specifically mentioned *"this generation?"* Some have argued that He was talking about the generation of His day that saw the destruction of the temple in 70 A.D. This cannot be so, because after saying that He said, *"till all these things take place."* What things? All of the things He had just mentioned regarding the end of those days, including the Day of His glorious return. Remember, this prophecy on the Mount of Olives was talking about two events, the most significant being His victorious earthly return of judgment and redemption.

Part Two—Section 2

When Jesus used the word "*generation,*" He gave those who understand a huge clue about the timing of His return. Many have tried to conclude how long a generation is. They have come up with periods of years such as 40, 52, 70, or the age gap between family offspring. That interpretation is far more complex than the simplicity of Jesus' own words. What Jesus meant, was that the generation would be alive to see the beginning of the signs and would still be alive at His return. He was describing the length of a person or people group's life span as the time for the length of the generation.

There can be no clearer interpretation in taking that whole passage in the context He meant to have it understood. Obviously, when He said "*generation,*" He was referring to a particular people group for a set period of time. That time frame has to have a specific start date and end date. At some point in the future, the end date will come and that generation He spoke of will be witness to His return. Only the Lord Himself knows what day and hour that will be. But, in understanding prophetic Scripture and modern history, we can likely know the day that the generation began. Again, for the Lord to have used the word "*generation,*" there has to be a specific start date and end date—an event in history that would mark the beginning of the "*generation.*"

Any Christian alive today with their eyes open to the world condition should be able to clearly discern that we are living in these last days spoken of by Jesus. What many don't realize, or maybe haven't thought about or understood, is the event in modern history that triggered the beginning of these last day signs and the start of the "*generation.*"

The generation that Jesus spoke of may have begun on May 14, 1948. This day in history marks the most significant prophetic event to be fulfilled since the first century. This prophecy is referenced throughout the Old Testament and New. It is the re-establishment of the nation of Israel.

On May 14, 1948 in a single day, God's chosen people were once again united as a nation in the land given to them by God—the land of their father's Abraham, Isaac, and Jacob. The everlasting covenant that God made with Abraham about his descendants and their land was resurrected on that day. This is something to get excited about! The reality of its implications is profound.

In about 721 B.C., the nation of Israel was conquered by the Assyrians, which continued a time of judgment on them for their rebellion against God. Their sister nation, Judah—the southern kingdom, held on for a while longer, but they too were eventually overthrown in 586 B.C. by the Babylonians. From then on, they were a people without a nation. Many Jews remained in the region and were ruled and controlled by numerous tyrants, kings, empires, and governments until they were totally vanquished from the land by the Romans in 70 A.D. After this, their land became more or less a barren and desolate wasteland.

In 1917, Great Britain, who gained control of the region from the Turks, decided the land should once again be occupied by their historic occupants, the Jews, who were literally dispersed throughout the entire world. The historic Balfour Declaration of 1917 encouraged Jews from around the world to migrate back to their homeland, known then as the British Mandate of Palestine. At that time, there were merely 40,000 Jews in the region. They began to migrate, and by end of WWII there were about 800,000 Jews back in their land.

Today, there are more than 7 million people in the nation of Israel. Israel has now clearly become the center of world attention. It has become a *"burdensome stone"* to nearly every nation of the world; just as the ancient prophet said it would be before Christ's return *(Zechariah 12:3)*. With the nation of Israel back in the land, Christ can now fulfill final prophecies as written by the Prophet Daniel. The 70th week, or seven year tribulation period, can now come to fruition. Christ once again has a nation and a people gathered to redeem, where He will rule and establish His earthly reign upon His return.

Many Bible scholars have come to understand that the *"fig tree"* mentioned in this parable is a direct symbolic reference to Israel itself.

There are many references in the Bible that do directly show the fig tree as a symbolic reference of divine judgment on Israel for her lack of spiritual fruit despite the abundant spiritual privileges given to them *(Hosea 9:10 and Joel 1:7).* One of the most striking references of this kind happened the day before Jesus had this discussion with His disciples on the mountain.

Beginning in *Matthew 21:18* is the story of Jesus cursing the fig tree. This is the only recorded miracle of Jesus that ever involved judgment. Jesus was hungry and saw a fig tree and came to it to eat, but found nothing on it but leaves. He then said to the tree, *"Let no fruit grow on you ever again."* The fig tree immediately withered away. Jesus' disciples saw this and were amazed at how quickly the tree had withered. Jesus was demonstrating the power of faith, but He was also illustrating God's judgment on the Israelites who proclaimed to follow God, but showed no fruit or spiritual evidence. Many of God's chosen people were about to reject and kill their awaited Messiah and would ultimately face severe judgment for that.

In understanding the parable of the fig tree, Jesus is telling us to watch for the re-budding of the "fig tree," symbolizing the rebirth of Israel. When we see this, we are to know this is the generation that will see His return. Read the parable again, because understanding this could be crucial to understanding the timing of the Lord's return.

> *Matthew 24:32-35 32 "Now learn this parable from the fig tree: When its branch has already become tender and puts forth leaves, you know that summer is near. 33 So you also, when you see all these things, know that it is near—at the doors! 34 Assuredly, I say to you, this generation will by no means pass away till all these things take place. 35 Heaven and earth will pass away, but My words will by no means pass away."*

Part Two—Section 3

It is clear that we are living in the time of the Lord's return and are the generation that will see His return, or be raptured from that time. There appears to be no other significant event, prophetic fulfillment, or date in modern history, other than May 14, 1948, that points to the start of the clock and the countdown for the beginning of the generation that will see the Lord's return. With that date established, the next logical question to answer is: "How long is a generation or a life span of a person supposed to be in these last days?" The best answer to questions like this are always found in the Scriptures. There is only one scripture in the entire Bible that specifically explains the answer to this question.

Psalm 90:10 states, *The days of our lives are seventy years; and if by reason of strength they are eighty years, yet their boast is only labor and sorrow; for it is soon cut off, and we fly away.* So, the Bible says our lives, on average, will last seventy years and if we are strong and healthy, eighty years. This gives us an average low figure and an average high figure to estimate the length of a generational lifespan.

If this scripture were the standard we were to use to gauge the length of a generation, then we would say, according to Scripture, a generation can be at most eighty years. It is interesting to note that the authorship of this Psalm falls upon none other than Moses, who himself lived to be 120 years old. It seems as if this verse may be prophetic in nature, because as time continued, life spans began to decrease. According to historians, by the time of King David's generation, seventy to eighty years of life was about the maximum and has continued to stay about the same through history up to our current generation. This does not take into consideration times in history of great war, plagues, and poor medical and sanitary conditions where you were lucky to live to the age of forty. This age of life falls more under a society where you have adequate sanitation, medical care and are able to live and die of more natural causes.

With a generation established at eighty years according to Scripture, would it be illogical to conclude that Christ would return no more than eighty years after the generation He spoke about began? Obviously it wouldn't seem likely that He would let the generation go to 120 years, 100 years, or even ninety years. Most people just do not live that long. That would be an unreasonable amount of time for a generation.

With Scripture backing the eighty year generation theory, this would be the most reasonable amount of time to anticipate for the generation Jesus spoke of in His parable. The point could then be made that since this generation seems to have begun in 1948, Christ would return to Earth no later than 2028. The seven year Tribulation would then begin in 2021.

This is not date setting such as stating a day or hour of His return, but more logical reasoning based on Scripture, or an educated guess. Could Christ come sooner than that? Absolutely. Could Christ come later than that? He certainly could if He wanted to, but would He? Remember, He's the one who gave us the clue about the generation that would not pass away. It would seem unlikely that He would carry out that generation beyond a reasonable number of years once it began.

If one were to make this argument regarding the timing of Christ's return based solely on the parable of the fig tree and the Olivet Discourse, it would certainly be compelling. But are there possibly more clues throughout Scripture that could support the hypothesis of an eighty year time period for a generation, or for the return of Christ eighty years after a 1948 starting point?

Part Two—Section 4

In understanding the nature of God and how He acts and reacts throughout biblical history, it could be said that if you want to know what God will do in the future, look at what He's done in the past. Consider how, throughout the Bible, the Lord has consistently used numbers that have significance to Him. Time and again, He uses numbers such as three, seven, and forty to name a few of the most common. The number seven and its compounds are used like no other number in the Bible and are used nearly 900 times. It is the number of perfection, or completion. The number forty is a number that represents times of probation, trial, and testing, as well as times of prosperity, deliverance, and waiting. It is used 146 times in the Scriptures.

God is very consistent in His use of numbers and number sequences. In understanding this, could it not be a possibility that God may use some of these same numbers for time periods of future prophetic events? We already know that there will be a seven year tribulation period, the final seven years of a 490 year period that Daniel prophesied about for the completion of Israel. This seven year period is also divided up into two, three and a half year periods. What about time periods that have not been set in Scripture that are future events, such as the amount of time between Israel's rebirth and Christ's return, or the time period between the Rapture and the Tribulation? These are time frames about which we are currently uninformed. Would it not be like the Lord to continue His pattern of using specific numbers for these time periods in the same way He has since the dawn of time?

Examine the life of Moses for example. He lived to be 120 years old and his life was divided into three distinct eras of forty years. He grew up for forty years in Egypt within Pharaoh's court, and then spent the next forty years in the wilderness of Midian as a sheep and goat farmer. His last forty years he spent delivering and leading the children of Israel out of Egypt and into the Promised Land. In this instance, Moses went from a time of prosperity and testing, to a time of probation and waiting, completing his life with times of deliverance and trial.

God used periods of forty years, compounded upon each other, to complete His perfect plan in the life of Moses. Look also at the time Moses was given the Ten Commandments. He went up onto Mount Sinai for forty days and received the law. He came back and destroyed the law, because of the people's sin, and then went back up on the mountain for forty more days receiving another set of commandments. This is another example of God using, in this case, two sets of the number forty to complete His goal. There are many more examples of God grouping numbers of forty together. Consider when the Israelites spied on the Promised Land for forty days coming back with a bad report and lack of faith, which resulted in a forty year punishment of wandering in the desert. An entire study could be done on God's use of the number forty in Scripture, especially in how it relates to His chosen people—Israel.

Part Two—Section 5

Having an understanding of the way God uses numbers, especially the number forty; would it not be like God to continue using that number in a special way in these last days, specifically towards Israel and the land they reclaimed in 1948? Certainly they have had times of prosperity, testing, and trials and we know from Scripture they are waiting for deliverance through Christ's redemption and unification of them into His kingdom upon His return.

From 1948 to 1988, the first forty years of their new nation, you can see them blessed, prospering in their land, and becoming a world super power. In fact, today they are one of the smallest nations on the earth, yet boast the world's fourth strongest military. They have had their problems no doubt, but you can clearly see the hand of the Lord protecting them and prospering them in areas of war and military might, agriculture, economics, culture, and technology. They have even rekindled the ancient lost language of Hebrew spoken by their ancestors, which is their national language. This in itself is seen as a last day's prophecy fulfilled (*Zephaniah 3:9*).

Beginning in about 1988 there began to be a shift of power in the region. The Iraq–Iran War ended in 1988 that had begun in 1980. Over 1.5 million people died during this war that engulfed the Middle East and had the world's attention. It seems as if the close of the war may have begun a renewed hatred for Israel. Their focus could be changed from fighting each other to again wanting to destroy God's people. The rise of the descendants of Ishmael and Esau, or the Muslim and Arab world, can be seen after the close of this war. God did promise Ishmael that his descendants would be mighty on the earth.

The Muslims have been powerful for centuries and have always hated the Jews, but in the last twenty-five years or so, the tide of power has begun to shift. Israel's neighbors have become more hostile and bent on Israel's total destruction than at any other time since their rebirth. There has been no greater threat to Israel from Ishmael's descendants than the situation that has developed there right now.

Just think about these recent Muslim inspired world events: the first Gulf War, September 11, 2001, the Iraq and Afghan Wars, the onslaught of missile attacks on Israel, global Islamic terrorism, the Arab Spring, the Syrian civil war, the persecution of Christians, and threats of nuclear annihilation for Israel. The Muslims now have a foothold in all the Middle East, Indonesia, North to Central Africa, Europe, the former Soviet Union, parts of Latin America, and even the U.S.A. Their grasp and sphere of influence on the Western world in these last days is alarming to say the least.

Upon examining past and current events, God may be breaking the timeline between Israel's rebirth and His return into two distinct eras of forty years. If God is doing this, He may return to establish His kingdom in the year 2028—eighty years after Israel's rebirth. In looking at modern history and God's way of using forty year fulfillments, this could very well be another clue being revealed in these last days regarding the timing of the return of our Lord. This eighty year pattern also seems to fit together with the eighty year generation theory from the "fig tree" parable.

Part Two—Section 6

Understanding the life of Moses and the deliverance of the Israelites from Egypt may be another clue revealing Christ's second coming. What does the birth of Moses and Israel's rebirth in 1948 have in common? Both births mark the beginning of a master plan for God to deliver and redeem His people. When Christ returns at the end of the Tribulation, this will be the second time God will have saved His people from bondage and destruction—the first being the exodus from Egypt through Moses.

Isaiah 11:11-16 is a prophetic verse that links these two redemptions together.

> *11 It shall come to pass in that day that the Lord shall set His hand again the second time to recover the remnant of His people who are left, from Assyria and Egypt, from Pathros and Cush, from Elam and Shinar, from Hamath and the islands of the sea. 12 He will set up a banner for the nations, and will assemble the outcasts of Israel, and gather together the dispersed of Judah from the four corners of the earth. 16 There will be a highway for the remnant of His people who will be left from Assyria, as it was for Israel in the day that he came up from the land of Egypt.*

Notice that verse eleven is describing the second time the Lord is recovering the remnant of His people. The second time was established on May 14, 1948 and will be fulfilled at Christ's second coming. The first time was established at the birth of Moses, and was fulfilled the day Israel came up from the land of Egypt as mentioned at the end of verse sixteen. Just like when Israel went from being slaves and in bondage into a mighty nation in one day—the day they were led out of Egypt, they again became a mighty nation in one day in May of 1948. These two events cannot be linked any more directly than as described in this particular passage of Scripture.

If you study the exodus from Egypt, looking at events that happened before, during, and after the exodus and compare that to prophecies concerning the last days and the second coming of Christ—God's ultimate redemption for Israel, you will find alarming symbolic similarities. Consider the chain of events that occurred when Moses first learned of God's plan to use him to deliver the Israelites.

- God met Moses in a powerful way to get his attention through a bush that was on fire, but was not burned up. God directly communicated to Moses with His spoken Word. Today, we are informed of Christ's second coming through prophecies in His written Word. The Bible was inspired upon man through the power of the Holy Spirit. In the Bible, fire is often a representation of the Holy Spirit as revealed on the day of Pentecost. And as the fiery bush was not destroyed, so we are promised that God's Word is eternal and will endure forever.

- In order for God to confirm His spoken Word to Moses and strengthen his faith, God showed Moses some miraculous signs as confirmation to what He had said. He turned Moses' staff into a serpent, and gave Moses a leprous hand then healed it instantly. God has given us prophetic signs in the Scriptures that are daily being fulfilled and have been since 1948 concerning the last days and the soon coming of the Lord. If that does not strengthen your faith and confirm His written Word, what will?

- When Moses and Aaron went into Egypt to carry out God's commands, God used plagues to torment and persuade Pharaoh to relent. Many of these same plagues God will use on the ungodly during the seven year tribulation period as prophesied in the book of Revelation.

- When God was pounding Egypt and Pharaoh with these plagues, for the most part, the children of Israel were protected and shielded from the destruction of the plagues. Similarly, during the time of the Tribulation, Christ's Church will not be here for this judgment, but will first be taken out in the Rapture. Also, the book of Revelation talks about a time during the Tribulation where a remnant of Israel will be hiding in a place of protection given to them by God where the Antichrist will not be able to harm them (Revelation 12). This is very symbolic to the Passover blood placed above the door posts in Egypt when the angel of death killed all the first born children, except for those who obeyed the direction of the Lord.

- When the children of Israel were led out of Egypt and were pursued by Pharaoh's army, God split the Red Sea in two, ultimately destroying the army and freeing the Israelites. When Christ returns at the end of the Tribulation, He too will show up in a big way. As Christ sets foot on the Mount of Olives, the mountain will literally split into two parts during a great earthquake. He will then ultimately destroy all His enemies in a display of His glorious power and great judgment redeeming Israel once again.

- Once the Israelites escaped and entered the wilderness, God was with them daily in a physical manifestation of a cloud by day and pillar of fire by night. He also took care of their every need, miraculously guiding them, feeding them, and revealing Himself to them continuously. When Christ returns and sets up His earthly millennial kingdom, Israel's redemption will be complete and prophecy will be fulfilled. He will be here physically to reign and rule as King. He will be their God and they will be His people and all of His children's needs will be met.

In understanding one of the most significant connections linking these two great events of redemption, you need to examine the amount of time it took from the initiation of God's plan, to the fulfillment of the plan that resulted in the children of Israel being delivered out of Egypt. In reading the first chapter of the book of Exodus, a picture is painted as to the condition that had befallen the Israelites in Egypt. The Israelites were abused, enslaved, and put in extreme bondage. They were feared by the Egyptians, because there were so many of them.

Exodus chapter two begins God's plan of redemption for the Israelites through the birth of Moses. Baby Moses' life was miraculously saved from certain death in Egypt. The divine plan went forth that not only rescued Moses and elevated him to a place of authority and respect, but ultimately rescued God's people.

At the age of forty, Moses was excommunicated from the Egyptians and left Egypt for asylum in Midian. At the conclusion of this season of Moses' life, God used him mightily. *Exodus 7:7* reads, *And Moses was eighty years old and Aaron eighty-three years old when they spoke to Pharaoh.* So, eighty years went by from the time Moses was born and God's plan was initiated, to the fulfillment of the redemption. Does that number sound familiar? This similarity cannot be ignored and may be one of the most significant clues in Scripture as to the timing of the Lord's return in these last days. These two plans of redemption are so similar in nature and purpose and are laid out clearly in Scripture, but for the most part have been overlooked as having significance for last day events.

Would it not be consistent with God's sovereign purposes that He may again use a period of eighty years for this final act of redemption at His return, as He did in the days of Moses? Could the answer to one of Bible prophecies most debated topics be so simple? We will one day soon find out.

Do not let the day May 14, 1948 escape your memory. There has been no other day in history that pinpoints the beginning day, just as the day Moses was born, for the ultimate redemption of God's people and fulfillment of the Great Day of Judgment. Our Lord and Savior Jesus Christ will return to this earth in power and glory to reign and rule with ultimate authority and justice.

Part Two—Section 7

Christ Returns in Glory and Judgment

Amos 4:13 For behold, He who forms mountains, and creates the wind, who declares to man what his thought is, and makes the morning darkness, who treads the high places of the earth—The Lord God of hosts is His name.

Isaiah 64:1,2 1 Oh, that you would rend the heavens and come down, that the mountains would tremble before you! 2 As when fire sets twigs ablaze and causes water to boil, come down to make your name known to your enemies and cause the nations to quake before you! NIV

Psalm 144:5 Part your heavens, Lord, and come down; touch the mountains, so that they smoke. NIV

Micah 1:3,4 3 Look! The Lord is coming from his dwelling place; he comes down and treads the heights of the earth. 4 The mountains melt beneath him and the valleys split apart, like wax before the fire, like water rushing down a slope. NIV

Isaiah 26:21 See, the Lord is coming out of his dwelling to punish the people of the earth for their sins. The earth will disclose the blood shed on it; the earth will conceal its slain no longer. NIV

Psalm 18:9 He parted the heavens and came down; dark clouds were under his feet. NIV

Habakkuk 3:6 He stood, and shook the earth; he looked, and made the nations tremble. The ancient mountains crumbled and the age-old hills collapsed—but he marches on forever. NIV

Zechariah 14:4 On that day his feet will stand on the Mount of Olives, east of Jerusalem, and the Mount of Olives will be split in two from east to west, forming a great valley, with half of the mountain moving north and half moving south. NIV

Isaiah 66 1 This is what the Lord says: "Heaven is my throne, and the earth is my footstool. Where is the house you will build for me? Where will my resting place be? 2 Has not my hand made all these things, and so they came into being?" declares the Lord. "These are the ones I look on with favor: those who are humble and contrite in spirit, and who tremble at my word. 3 But whoever sacrifices a bull is like one who kills a person, and whoever offers a lamb is like one who breaks a dog's neck; whoever makes a grain offering is like one who presents pig's blood, and whoever burns memorial incense is like one who worships an idol. They have chosen their own ways, and delight in their abominations; 4 so I also will choose harsh treatment for them and will bring on them what they dread. For when I called, no one answered, when I spoke, no one listened. They did evil in my sight and chose what displeases me." 5 Hear the word of the Lord, you who tremble at his word: "Your own people who hate you, and exclude you because of my name, have said, 'Let the Lord be glorified, that we may see your joy!' Yet they will be put to shame. 6 Hear the uproar from the city, hear that noise from the temple! It is the sound of the Lord repaying his enemies all they deserve. 7 "Before she goes into labor, she gives birth; before the pain comes upon her, she delivers a son. 8 Who has ever heard of such things? Who has ever seen things like this? Can a country be born in a day or a nation be brought forth in a moment? Yet no sooner is Zion in labor than she gives birth to her children. 9 Do I bring to the moment of birth and not give delivery?" says the Lord. "Do I close up the womb when I bring to delivery?" says your God. 10 "Rejoice with Jerusalem and be glad for her, all you who love her; rejoice greatly with her, all you who mourn over her. 11 For you will nurse and be satisfied at her comforting breasts; you will drink deeply and delight in her overflowing abundance." 12 For this is what the Lord says: "I will extend peace to her like a river, and the wealth of the nations like a flooding stream; you will nurse and be carried on her arm and dandled on her knees. 13 As a mother comforts her child, so will I comfort you; and you will be comforted over Jerusalem." 14 When you see this, your heart will rejoice and you will flourish like grass; the hand of the Lord will be made known to his servants, but his fury will be shown to his foes. 15 See, the Lord is coming with fire, and his chariots are like a whirlwind; he will bring down his anger with fury, and his rebuke with flames of fire. 16 For with fire and with his sword the Lord will execute judgment on all people, and many will be those slain by the Lord. 17 "Those who consecrate and purify themselves to go into the gardens, following one who is among those who eat the flesh of pigs, rats and other unclean things—they will meet their end together with the one they follow," declares the Lord. 18 "And I, because of what they have planned and done, am about to come and gather the people of all nations and languages, and they will come and see my glory. 19 "I will set a sign among them, and I will send some of those who survive to the nations—to Tarshish, to the Libyans and Lydians, to Tubal and Greece, and to the distant islands that have not heard of my fame or seen my glory. They will proclaim my glory among the nations. 20 And they will bring all your people, from all the nations, to my holy mountain in Jerusalem as an offering to the Lord—on horses, in chariots and wagons, and on mules and camels," says the Lord. "They will bring them, as the Israelites bring the grain offerings, to the temple of the Lord in ceremonially clean vessels. 21 And I will select some of them also to be priests and Levites," says the Lord. 22 "As the new heavens and the new earth that I will make endure before me," declares the Lord, "so will your name and descendants endure. 23 From one New Moon to another and from one Sabbath to another, all mankind will come and bow down before me," says the Lord. 24 "And they will go out and look on the dead bodies of those who rebelled against me; the worms that eat them will not die, the fire that burns them will not be quenched, and they will be loathsome to all mankind." NIV

Revelation 19:11-16 11 Now I saw heaven opened, and behold, a white horse. And He who sat on him was called Faithful and True, and in righteousness He judges and makes war. 12 His eyes were like a flame of fire, and on His head were many crowns. He had a name written that no one knew except Himself. 13 He was clothed in a robe dipped in blood, and His name is called The Word of God. 14 And the armies in heaven, clothed in fine linen, white and clean, followed Him on white horses. 15 Now out of his mouth goes a sharp sword, that with it He should strike the nations. And He Himself will rule them with a rod of iron. He Himself treads the winepress of the fierceness and wrath of Almighty God. 16 And He has on His robe and on His thigh a name written: KING OF KINGS AND LORD OF LORDS.

Part Three

Imminency

Understanding the Timing of the Rapture

Section 1

Since Christ ascended into heaven nearly 2000 years ago, His Church has been awaiting His imminent return. The Rapture, when He comes to take His followers home, is not to be confused with His final return to earth at the end of the Tribulation. His final return will not be an imminent event, but will be expected, likely known as to the approximate day He returns. It will not be imminent due to the fact His return will be at the end of the seven year Tribulation as prophesied in the Bible. These days are numbered and are clearly laid out in the books of Daniel and Revelation. When Jesus said no one would know the day or hour of His return, He was probably referencing the timing of the Rapture. Though expected, it is quite possible the exact day of His return at the end of the Tribulation will also be unknown.

In order to better understand Christ coming to this world, think of Him coming in three parts: His first coming and incarnation, the Rapture, and then His final triumphant return. The problem the Jews had in not recognizing His first coming was that many of the prophetic scriptures they were wanting to focus on was the description of His final coming. They more or less ignored the ones describing His first coming. They liked the scriptures that tickled their ears regarding His triumphant defeat of their enemies at the end of the Tribulation. Many disregarded the prophecies concerning Him coming as a humble, sacrificial servant that would ultimately die for the transgression of man's sin (Isaiah chapter 53).

In the Bible, for every one prophetic verse describing Christ's first coming there are about eight others that mention His second coming. In studying the New Testament regarding the second coming, many scriptures reference Him coming to rescue and remove His Church from wrath as it describes the Rapture. Other scriptures refer to His triumphant and final return. One return describes Him descending into the clouds where He meets His faithful believers at the Rapture and Resurrection. The other return describes Him coming with great authority and power where all see Him and He physically touches down on planet earth, specifically the Mount of Olives east of Jerusalem. Both returns are clearly two distinct and different events in nature and purpose. There are even a few verses in the Old Testament that may allude to the Rapture of the Church for divine protection, though the Church was an unknown mystery at that time (*Isaiah 26:19-21, Zephaniah 2:3, Psalm 27:5*).

Consider the following illustration as a mental picture to understand how Christ will return in these last days.

Revelation 3:20 Behold, I stand at the door and knock. If anyone hears My voice and opens the door, I will come in to him and dine with him, and he with Me.

Mark 13:29 So you also, when you see these things happening, know that it is near—at the doors!

Revelation 4:1 After these things I looked, and behold, a door standing open in heaven. And the first voice which I heard was like a trumpet speaking with me, saying, "Come up here, and I will show you things which must take place after this."

Imagine a large door in heaven and Christ standing behind the door ready to open it. When it is fully open He will come out and return in glory. Picture seeing a door handle turn as the door cracks open. As the crack gets wider, you see a nail scarred hand reaching out and down. All of the sudden, His arm emerges; a trumpet sounds and His voice says, "Come up here." His arm plunges to the earth and snatches all the believers from the earth, grabs them and carries them up through the crack in the door and into the gates of heaven at the Rapture.

Once the believers are rescued and secure, the door opens further and out comes a nail scarred foot. This time the purpose will not be a rescue mission, but a slaughter and war victory. The door flies open and the Lord Jesus Christ and His armies descend to the earth with fire in His eyes and wrath and vengeance on His mind. With His foot He will crush Satan, the Antichrist, and all who oppose Him.

The Lord is patient and He gives plenty of opportunity for repentance as the door handle of time turns. But the day will come where He must take action and relent in His restraint. That is the time we are now living in. His hand is emerging from the door and is about to lunge forth and pull us out in the Rapture. It is a time to be sober, yet get excited! We're almost out of here! No other event in history needs to take place for the Rapture to happen. The time is imminent. It is "at the doors" and could happen at any moment.

Many have tried to find the word "Rapture" in the Bible and have come to the conclusion that it's not in there. The word "Rapture" is actually in the Bible, just not in an English translation. We get our word "Rapture" from the Latin word "Rapturo," which you will find in a Latin version of the Bible. Rapturo literally means to be caught up, seized, or taken by force. In Greek biblical texts the word Harpazo is used. The Greek translation for Harpazo is understood as "to seize upon with force" or "to snatch up." No matter which word you use—Rapturo, Harpazo, or our English word "Rapture," the meaning and nature of this event is all the same.

You will find one of the most descriptive and convincing scriptures regarding the Rapture in *1 Thessalonians 4:13-18*. This passage of Scripture describes the Lord descending into the clouds bringing with Him the dead believers who are now in heaven clothed in temporary spirit bodies. These believers are miraculously united with their old earthly bodies and are resurrected. Then we believers who are alive are "caught up" (raptured) in the air with them to meet the Lord in the clouds. It is at this time that Christ's Church (dead or alive) will receive their new resurrected, imperishable, eternal, physical bodies similar in nature to Christ's resurrected body. We will all be ushered into heaven by Christ.

Followers of Christ alive on the earth at the Rapture will never taste death, but will be transformed in a moment into glorious, eternal human beings with unimaginable abilities *(1 Corinthians 15:50-55)*. Though we more often refer to this wondrous event as the "Rapture," probably a more accurate and biblical word for this is called the

"Resurrection." This is what the multitudes in heaven are eagerly awaiting as they anticipate their final redemption and glorification when they will be resurrected eternally whole and complete.

An easy way to understand the Rapture is to think of it in terms of the concept of "translation," being transported instantaneously from one place to another—supernatural transportation. The idea of translation or Rapture is not a one-time event in the Bible, but throughout the Bible there are several "Raptures," or translation events that have and will occur.

Consider these famous Bible Rapture events: Enoch, Elijah, Phillip, Paul, John, Jesus, the Church, and the two witnesses from the book of Revelation. Each of these had, or will have an individually specific Rapture occurrence where they are divinely transported to heaven or some other location in an instant. As one can see, the idea of the "Rapture" is not just specific to what we're looking towards, but is something the Lord has used for His sovereign purposes throughout history. Undoubtedly, the Rapture we will experience will be the largest, most miraculous and wonderful display of God's power and intervention on humanity that has ever occurred.

Also, think about other symbolic "Rapture" events where God saved His people. The idea of God saving His righteous people from judgment is not foreign to His ways. He spared Noah and his family from the flood, as well as Lot and his family in Sodom, and Rahab and her family at the siege of Jericho. In fact, some view Enoch's departure as a pre-flood Rapture sparing him from that judgment, similar to a Pre-tribulation Rapture. The notion that God will save His Bride—the Church, from His wrath during the Tribulation is right in line with His past dealings with mankind and a tribute to His mercy and grace. Again, if you want to know what God will likely do in the future, just look at what He's done in the past.

Part Three—Section 2

The doctrine of imminency is a biblical belief that the Lord could return for His Church at the Rapture at any moment. This belief has been around since the day Christ ascended into the clouds and His disciples were given instruction by two angels as they stared up into the sky. They were told that Christ would be returning in the manner that He left (*Acts 1:9-11*).

A good definition of imminent would be: impending, likely to occur at any moment, about to happen very soon, approaching, or the time is at hand. The belief that Christ was anticipated to return at any moment is what drove the first century Church to pursue a lifestyle of righteousness and holiness unto the Lord, expecting that He would find them serving Him whole heartedly upon His return. This is the same reason we should be zealous in serving the Lord today.

James, the half-brother of Jesus and author of what is considered the first book to have been written in the New Testament, was well aware of the Lord's imminent return and soon coming.

> *James 5:7-9 7 Therefore be patient, brethren, until the coming of the Lord. See how the farmer waits for the precious fruit of the earth, waiting patiently for it until it receives the early and latter rain. 8 You also be patient. Establish your hearts, for the coming of the Lord is at hand.*

Consider other verses showing the early Church's expectancy of the Lord's soon coming.

> *1 Peter 4:7 But the end of all things is at hand; therefore be serious and watchful in your prayers.*

> *Titus 2:11-13 11 For the grace of God that brings salvation has appeared to all men, 12 teaching us that, denying ungodliness and worldly lusts, we should live soberly, righteously, and godly in the*

present age, 13 looking for the blessed hope and glorious appearing of our great God and Savior Jesus Christ.

Romans 13:11-12 11 And do this, knowing the time, that now it is high time to awake out of sleep; for now our salvation is nearer than when we first believed. 12 The night is far spent, the day is at hand. Therefore let us cast off the works of darkness, and let us put on the armor of light.

Hebrews 10:24,25,37 24 And let us consider one another in order to stir up love and good works, 25 not forsaking the assembling of ourselves together, as is the manner of some, but exhorting one another, and so much the more as you see the Day approaching. 37 "For yet a little while, And He who is coming will come and will not tarry.

1 John 2:18 Little children, it is the last hour; and as you have heard that the Antichrist is coming, even now many antichrists have come, by which we know that it is the last hour.

Revelation 22:7,20 7 "Behold, I am coming quickly! Blessed is he who keeps the words of the prophecy of this book." 20 He who testifies to these things says, "Surely I am coming quickly." Amen. Even so, come, Lord Jesus!

It does not appear that these first century followers of Jesus were looking forward to seeing Christ return at the end of a seven year period of wrath. What they were anticipating was *"looking for the blessed hope and glorious appearing."*

The Apostle Paul in his letters to the church in Thessalonica went to great lengths to clear up an issue the church had in regards to the Rapture and final return of Jesus. The Thessalonians had gotten hold of some false teaching. Many believed that they had missed the Rapture and were already in the apocalyptic period of the Tribulation, because of the severe trials they were facing.

In *2 Thessalonians 2:1,2* Paul encourages the church.

> *1 Now, brethren, concerning the coming of our Lord Jesus Christ and our gathering together to Him,* (notice two events) *we ask you, 2 not to be soon shaken in mind or troubled, either by spirit or by word or letter, as if from us, as though the day of Christ had come.*

Paul went on to explain that the "Day" would not come until the "falling away"—the great apostasy of the Church, and the Antichrist defiled himself in the temple of God. Paul was reassuring them that they were not in the Tribulation, to relax and not worry.

In *1 Thessalonians 5* Paul reassured them by saying:

> 1 *But concerning the times and the seasons, brethren, you have no need that I should write to you. 2 For you yourselves know perfectly that the day of the Lord so comes as a thief in the night. 6 Therefore let us not sleep, as others do, but let us watch and be sober. 9 For God did not appoint us to wrath, but to obtain salvation through our Lord Jesus Christ...*

Paul is explaining that they already know when Christ comes for them it will be at an unexpected time, like a thief coming in the night. He tells them to not worry, just be on alert and watching, because God will come for them and spare them from His wrath that He will pour out upon the earth.

The doctrine of imminency shatters any ideas or beliefs that the Church will be subject to God's vengeance and wrath during the Tribulation. If you don't believe in the imminency of His return, then you should be watching for the rise of the Antichrist, world turmoil, and horrific judgments to fall upon the earth. That scenario does not sound like a "blessed hope," or something to be encouraged about. If you come to faith after Christ comes for His Bride in the Rapture, then that certainly will be your reality.

In studying the book of Revelation, you will get an idea of just how cataclysmic and earth shattering the judgments will be during the Tribulation. According to the numbers given in Revelation for those who die during this time, half the world's population will die in the first three and a half years alone. Two thirds of the Jews will die during the last half of the Tribulation—The Great Tribulation. In all, it is likely that at least seventy-five percent of all the people on the earth will have been killed by the time Christ returns.

This time is specifically meant as a purging of the ungodly and a rebuke on Israel that will ultimately convince them that Christ is their Messiah who has come to redeem them. It will also be a time of great repentance and faith in Christ, but most will be martyred and suffer horrendous persecution for the Truth. Truly, only a remnant of humanity, believers and unbelievers alike, will survive the Tribulation to see the Lord's return.

One may ask how the early Church could have been in the last days, if two thousand years later Christ still has not come. How could that time have been considered the "last days?" The entire church age is considered the "last days." Time for us is not the same as is it for God. This dispensation or period we are now in—the age of grace—the times of the gentiles—the church age—whatever you wish to call it, these last two thousand years are the final days for Christ to complete His work upon the earth prior to His coming. The Apostle Peter could not have answered this question any better.

> 2 Peter 3:8,9 8 But, beloved, do not forget this one thing, that with the Lord one day is as a thousand years, and a thousand years as one day. 9 The Lord is not slack concerning His promise, as some count slackness, but is longsuffering toward us, not willing that any should perish but that all should come to repentance.

These are the last days. During this time the Lord has been patient, allowing opportunity for as many as possible to choose to follow Him. His desire for all is that many would repent and receive the gift of pardon that Christ has to offer through His sacrifice for sin that was paid for on the cross. For whoever will believe, will have the right to be called children of the Living God. It is these children of God brought up during these days who will be spared from God's wrath about to be poured out upon the earth in the near future.

Part Three—Section 3

The last two thousand years have been hard for Christ's Church. At times persecution has been rampant. There have been an untold number of believers who have died horrible deaths at the hands of evil men. But has there ever been a time where God has poured out His wrath on His Church, or let alone the world during this time? No, He has not. There is only one instance in Scripture that declares the time when He will pour out His wrath. That is the time of the Tribulation.

There is no doubt that God has judged His children and the world at times for His sovereign purposes and correction, but there is a stark contrast to the ways God has dealt with us and the unimaginable judgment to be released during the Tribulation. Christ's Church has not been appointed to wrath. Christ will spare His Church from that time just as He did in the days of Noah. The Holy Spirit's hand of restraint has been upon the earth, but that restraint is about to be lifted.

The Apostle Paul explained to the church at Thessalonica that the restraining power of the Holy Spirit would be removed prior to the rise of the Antichrist. This is one of the most solid passages of Scripture in the Bible clearly showing the Church will not be present during the Tribulation, or be here to see the rise of the Antichrist.

> 2 Thessalonians 2:6-8 *6 And now you know what is restraining, that he* (Antichrist) *may be revealed in his own time. 7 For the mystery of lawlessness is already at work; only He* (Holy Spirit) *who now restrains will do so until He is taken out of the way. 8 And then the lawless one will be revealed, whom the Lord will consume with the breath of His mouth and destroy with the brightness of His coming.*

Who in the entire universe has the power and authority to restrain evil, or restrain the rise of the Antichrist? Of course the answer is God, through the power and working of the Holy Spirit. Believer, you know that you are a temple of the Holy Spirit. God dwells inside you.

We have no idea what kind of evil we are restraining in this world through our prayers and power of the Holy Spirit, or even our mere presence on the earth. If the Holy Spirit and His power of restraint is "taken out of the way," then guess what? We are no longer here. We were just raptured! The Holy Spirit's restraint cannot be taken out of the way without His host, the believer, also being taken out of the way. "Taken out of the way" sure sounds like one of the definitions given for "Rapturo" and "Harpazo."

The Antichrist is restrained from rising to power until after the Rapture. Our removal gives him the green light and ability to do what he is meant to do. This scripture assures you that not only will you not know who the Antichrist is, but you will not be present for any of the judgments of the Tribulation. Halleluiah!

The Holy Spirit will still be working and influencing mankind during the Tribulation, but His function of restraining evil will be lifted for that time. As new believers emerge during the Tribulation, the Holy Spirit will be essential in comforting, strengthening, and guiding them through that difficult time. Unfortunately for the believer, at times death will be seen as a gift and an escape from hell on earth to glory during those horrific days.

Part Three—Section 4

In conversations there are questions that are frequently asked about the Rapture and Tribulation with often uncertain answers. One question is: "How long do you think the Rapture will happen before the Tribulation begins?" A common answer is: "The Rapture will happen right before the Tribulation." That idea is not necessarily based on Scripture, but would be more of an assumption or what someone else has said.

Another question is: "What do you think starts the Tribulation?" Common answers for that are: "The Rapture starts the Tribulation. Or, the rise of the Antichrist starts the Tribulation." Both of those answers would be incorrect. Neither starts the Tribulation, but the latter is closer to the correct answer. What the Antichrist does and is able to accomplish will start the Tribulation, though his world dominating empire will likely be emerging when it happens.

Day one of the seven year Tribulation begins when the Antichrist establishes a seven year peace treaty or "covenant" with the nation Israel. When this happens, you can know for certain that the world leader that made this possible is none other than the Antichrist. You will find this future prophetic information in the book of Daniel chapter 9 as you study the "Seventy-Weeks Prophecy."

The entire book of Daniel is a work of prophetic wonder as the Lord, through Daniel, proclaims history from his time through the first and then second coming of Christ. The prophecies in the book of Daniel are so profound that skeptics have claimed them to be a fraud. They say the book could not have possibly been written and predicted with such accuracy hundreds of years before events came to pass. But it is no fraud. Its message is absolutely crucial in understanding the timing and purpose of the Tribulation and the role of the Antichrist during that time.

In a nutshell, the "Seventy Weeks Prophecy" is a time period given to Daniel by the angel Gabriel that reveals the final years established for the Lord's people—Israel. The purpose is spelled out in *Daniel 9:24.*

> "Seventy weeks are determined for your people and for your holy city, to finish the transgression, to make an end of sins, to make reconciliation for iniquity, to bring in everlasting righteousness, to seal up vision and prophecy, and to anoint the Most Holy.

Seventy weeks means seventy "weeks of years," not seventy calendar weeks. Each week represents seven years, or one day equals one year (70 times 7) for a total of 490 years. This is based on the ancient 360 day calendar year, not our current calendar system.

> Daniel 9:25-27 25 "Know therefore and understand, that from the going forth of the command to restore and build Jerusalem until Messiah the Prince, there shall be seven weeks and sixty-two weeks; the street shall be built again, and the wall, even in troublesome times. 26 "And after the sixty-two weeks Messiah shall be cut off, but not for Himself; and the people of the prince who is to come shall destroy the city and the sanctuary. The end of it shall be with a flood, and till the end of the war desolations are determined. 27 Then he shall confirm a covenant with many for one week; but in the middle of the week He shall bring an end to sacrifice and offering. And on the wing of abominations shall be one who makes desolate, even until the consummation, which is determined, is poured out on the desolate."

From looking at history, the first seven weeks began on March 14, 445 B.C. when the command went forth to restore and rebuild Jerusalem *(Nehemiah 2)*. It was completed exactly forty-nine years later—the first seven weeks. At the time it was finished, the clock started for the beginning of the next sixty-two weeks, or 434 years. The 434 years came to completion the day Jesus was paraded through the streets of Jerusalem before His crucifixion. When Israel rejected their Messiah and Christ went to the cross, the clock stopped. There is yet the last week or seven years to be fulfilled—the time of the Tribulation.

As verse 27 points out, the Antichrist starts the 70th week when he confirms a "covenant" for "one week," or seven years. The day this covenant is established is day one of the seven year Tribulation. When the clock stopped at Christ's rejection by Israel, God shifted His focus and began the "times of the Gentiles," or the church age—the age we are now living in. He has not forgotten His promises to Israel. Christ will once again focus on Israel during the 70th week to complete His final work for them as laid out in verse 24.

Part Three—Section 5

Many speculate the Rapture will happen just before the Tribulation. That is speculation at best with really not giving much thought into what has to happen before the start of the Tribulation. We know that the Rapture will happen prior to the revealing of the Antichrist. We know the Antichrist will have to be a well-established and respected world leader in order to solve the Middle East peace conflict in one day as he establishes a seven year peace treaty with Israel.

World leaders don't generally rise to power in an instant—they have to prove themselves, form alliances, gain a following and establish their rule. The Antichrist will essentially rule the world or will have the most powerful empire in the world. He won't do this overnight. Again, before the Rapture the world will not have a clue about who this leader is. The Rapture is likely the event that hurls him to center stage, or at least causes him to rise in some degree.

There is no mention of the United States of America or anything similar to her as a world power in the Bible during the time of the Tribulation or rule of the Antichrist. As being the world's current superpower, it can only be assumed that this country will lose its footing in the world.

Imagine the U.S.A. as it has been the last couple hundred years just handing the reigns over to a foreign power. This country will have to be crippled severely and be brought to her knees for the Antichrist to rise and accomplish what Scripture says he will do. Just look at our country now. The ground work is already in place as our alliances with the United Nations and other foreign entities have strengthened with the goal of forming a one world alliance. Our economy is heavily damaged from lavish spending and poor policies. The nation is experiencing the breakdown of the family with a morally destitute people majority. Our country meets all the biblical criteria necessary for God to dismantle a nation such as ours and we have done it to ourselves as a result of falling away from the biblical truth our nation was founded on. But this is all a part of God's sovereign plan.

One can only speculate what event or events will cause our destruction. Some think a nuclear bomb or EMP (electro-magnetic pulse) attack, cyber warfare, economic collapse, or a natural disaster such as a West Coast subduction quake and tsunami may bring us down. We could likely survive a nuclear attack or tsunami, but could our nation survive the Rapture?

Just imagine the moment our nation loses 20 to 40 million or more of its citizens in an instant. Christians are truly the salt and light of this nation and are embedded in all forms of society. We are the bedrock that stabilizes this country morally and spiritually. Our presence in this country is a major restraining force against evil and the attack of Satan here and around the world. When we vanish, all hell will break loose around this country for a time—anarchy, looting, murder, suicide, theft, drug and alcohol abuse will all spiral out of control. Lawlessness will be uncontrollable. It will be a shock to the senses and those left behind will not be able to cope. Not to mention possibly one of the most disturbing aspects of the Rapture for those not taken—the loss of the children.

There are two biblical theories about this topic; one being that all children under the age of accountability, whatever that age is for each person, will be Raptured. The other thought is that only children with believing parents or a believing parent will be taken and the children of unbelievers will be left. Both camps have Scripture to back up their views, but the Bible just does not definitively say what happens to the children at the Rapture. There will be children taken in the Rapture, just which ones are up for debate. Imagine if all the children do go and unbelieving parents watch their children vanish before their very eyes, or find them missing from their beds. The despair, panic, depression, frustration, and anger they will face is unimaginable. What happens to the unbelieving mother who is pregnant if the baby vanishes from the womb? Does she bleed out internally from the severed connection? What horror!

Now top off the repercussions of the Rapture with the evil plans of opportunist countries that hate us like Iran and North Korea. Would they throw a couple nukes our way and kick us while we're down? Wouldn't that also be an inopportune time for that tsunami to hit, or for China to hack our computer grid and infrastructure to the point of collapse? After the Rapture, our country could collapse and all that would be left is a former shadow of the nation. Most of this would likely happen before the Tribulation ever begins. The American dream would consist of people trying to protect their lives and property, while finding ways to survive as immoral marauders rape and pillage the country. Martial law will rule the day. Now as bad as that sounds, that too will not happen overnight after the Rapture. It will take time for complete collapse.

When the Antichrist rises you can be assured that the U.S.A. will eagerly seek what he has to offer as he takes us under his wings, or finishes us off. It could be our pillaged resources that help build his mighty empire. The sting of the Rapture will undoubtedly affect every nation of the earth negatively, but is there any other nation on the planet that has more to lose or has a bigger Christian influence than the United States? Is there any other nation on the planet that is hated or envied more than the United States? According to the Muslims of the world, we are the "Great Satan" and first on the list that needs to be annihilated, followed by Israel the "little Satan."

Here's what Jesus had to say about the day of the Rapture: *For it will come as a snare on all those who dwell on the face of the whole earth (Luke 21:35).* When the Christians leave this planet, one can only imagine what havoc that will wreak on the world community. You do not want to be left behind to experience this judgment.

Part Three—Section 6

There is a high likelihood that after the Rapture of the Church there could be a significant amount of time that may pass before the Tribulation begins. The Rapture does not start the Tribulation. In understanding God's use of time throughout history for events and periods that involve His people and plans, would it not be like God to again use a specific number of years for His purposes in establishing a specific time period between the Rapture and the Tribulation? We can be confident that it won't be a number of years such as eighty or forty, which are all numbers God has used in the past. Those periods of time are too unreasonably long. They just don't fall into what Scripture reveals about God's time table for the generation that will see His return. What about seven or three and a half years? Both of those numbers have significance to God, especially the number seven, the number of perfection and completion.

The number three and a half is significant in the Tribulation as the Tribulation is divided into two, three and a half year time periods. Three and a half years should be enough time for America to collapse and for the Antichrist to rise to power causing the events that start the Tribulation after the Rapture. Although three and a half years may seem like a reasonable amount of time God would use for this future period, seven years may definitely be a more logical number of years between the Rapture and Tribulation.

The number seven appears to be God's favorite number as it is used nearly 900 times in the Bible. God uses a period of seven years for His divine judgment on the earth during the Tribulation. May it be that God would also use a time period of seven years for His saints to celebrate and experience the city of heaven prior to the start of the Tribulation? This idea just seems logical.

We know that at some point once the Rapture and Resurrection occur and we are all in glory, that we will participate in the Marriage Supper of the Lamb and the Judgment Seat of Christ (Bema Judgment).

We will all receive our eternal rewards and placement into Christ's eternal kingdom. These events will not happen instantly, but will happen over a period of time in heaven where there will be worship, praise, celebration, fulfillment, completion, placement, introduction, instruction, exploration, rejuvenation, and reconciliation. Words can't describe, nor can our minds even grasp what that time will be like when all that we have been waiting for begins to happen. Would it not be like our Heavenly Father to use His favorite number to complete and perfect His Bride during a seven year time period before the start of the Tribulation? The celebration and feast may last longer than that, but seven years would sure be a good start for God to place us into His eternal kingdom.

Our introduction into heaven and our gathering together with saints that have already passed at the Resurrection will be an event that will encompass all of heaven. It's what believers currently in heaven have been waiting for and what we are also looking forward to. Though God certainly could accomplish both at the same time, do you think this special reunion and Marriage Supper will coincide with the Tribulation judgments? It would seem to make sense for the Marriage Supper and Bema Judgment to occur prior to the Tribulation. Just as Christ will judge the earth for seven years, His Marriage Feast could also last seven years before judgment begins.

Another way to look at this is to understand what is going on in heaven during the time of the Tribulation. The book of Revelation explains in detail many of the events that are occurring in heaven and in God's throne room during this time. The Apostle John sees this future period unfold before his eyes. What John is witnessing is angels, martyred Tribulation saints, and other heavenly creatures worshipping God and observing the horrors of the judgments on the earth. Martyred saints are crying out to God wondering how long the Lord will tarry in putting an end to the evil and persecution of the saints. In fact, at one point there is silence in heaven for thirty minutes before God pours out some of the worst of the judgments on the earth.

Heaven, God's throne room, Jesus, angels, and Tribulation saints are all clearly involved in the events of the Tribulation. One would not speculate that at that same time the Church is also enjoying a great feast with Jesus, or participating in the Bema judgment. We certainly could be, but Scripture does not say that. It would seem unlikely. Remember, the Church and His saints are returning with the Lord Jesus at the end of the Tribulation to assist in establishing His millennial reign. One would only assume that our rewards or lack of would have already been issued and the marriage feast had been completed. This is only an assumption at best. It could be that during the Tribulation we are being prepared or trained in some way for our role in Christ's return and participation in His millennial reign. Or, we could be exploring and experiencing the joys of heaven, or both. One can only imagine.

Part Three—Section 7

Consider if you will, a passage of Scripture from the book of 1 Kings chapters eight and nine, which may shed some light on the period of time between the Rapture and Christ's return to earth. In understanding this passage of Scripture and how it may relate to end time prophecy, you will need to examine it with a symbolic mindset. The illustration is totally based on symbolism and may be an inference or foreshadowing of a future event. Again, this passage of Scripture does not state these events will transpire according to this time table. It is not something we will know unless it actually happens this way in the future. Nonetheless, grasping what this Scripture may be revealing is certainly worth thinking about.

In the book of 1 Kings you learn of how King David proclaimed his son Solomon as the next King of Israel near the time of his death. Solomon rose to power and had a visitation and conversation with God in the form of a dream. God was pleased with Solomon, because the new king loved the Lord and was walking with the Lord as his father David had, except that he sacrificed and burned incense at the high places (*1 Kings 3:3*). Regardless of that, the Lord appeared to Solomon and offered him an amazing gift. God offered to give to Solomon whatever he asked for. Solomon chose wisely and asked the Lord for wisdom in judging and leading his people. God was pleased with the request, and in addition to wisdom God chose to bless Solomon with riches and honor. This was God's first appearance to Solomon in a dream, but God later appeared to Solomon a second time.

Solomon received wisdom, riches, and honor and led his people wisely just as God had promised. Solomon then began the construction of the first temple fulfilling God's promise to King David. The blue print for the temple had been supernaturally given by God to King David and then passed down to King Solomon. Construction began in the fourth year of Solomon's reign (966 B.C.), which was four hundred and eighty years after the children of Israel were led out of Egypt (1445 B.C.).

Solomon built an elaborate house for the Lord that was likely the world's greatest wonder at that time. It was exquisite. The very temple itself was symbolic of God's temple in heaven. This temple was a place where God's presence could dwell with mankind on Earth. Building the temple took seven years. When it was finished, Solomon then proceeded to build his own house and other houses and structures on the temple grounds. All the other construction that Solomon did took thirteen years. In all, it took twenty years for the temple and other buildings to be completed.

When all the construction was done, the Lord visited Solomon a second time in a dream. During this visitation, the Lord promised Solomon that as long as Israel was led according to the Lord's direction and as long as Solomon obeyed the Lord and walked in His ways, the Lord would establish his throne and kingdom forever. But if Solomon or his sons turned from the Lord, disobeyed Him and worshipped other gods, the Lord would judge the nation, the temple would be destroyed, and calamity would fall on the people.

If you compare these two appearances of God to Solomon to Christ's first coming and then His second coming, you will notice strong symbolic similarities. In His first appearance to Solomon, God gave Solomon a precious gift that he never really deserved. In like manner, Christ came to the earth and offered Himself to humanity as payment for man's sin, when man did not deserve this gift. When God visited Solomon the second time, He offered Solomon and his throne salvation and an eternal kingdom, yet warned of judgment for rebelling against the Lord. Similarly, when Christ returns at the end of the Tribulation He will offer redemption and salvation for the remnant of His people who have survived and those who are following Him at His return. As He establishes His eternal throne on the earth, He will likewise judge the surviving wicked who have rebelled against Him.

Whether or not these similarities have any prophetic or symbolic relevance can be debated. One thing that can be understood is that God has shown us that He passionately desires to bless and honor all those who honor and obey Him. He also reveals that He will judge, correct, and discipline those who rebel and dishonor Him. This was demonstrated in the life of Solomon and the authority to bless and judge is clearly seen in Christ.

This next passage of Scripture may paint a picture of a future possibility involving the timing of the Rapture. Solomon just completed the temple, gives a magnificent speech, and blesses the people. He then prays and dedicates the temple to the Lord. After this, Solomon holds a great feast and celebration. In addition to the plain interpretation of this passage, imagine a possible future foreshadowing.

> *1 Kings 8:65,66 65 At that time Solomon held a feast, and all Israel with him, a great assembly from the entrance of Hamath to the Brook of Egypt, before the Lord our God, seven days and seven more days—fourteen days. 66 On the eighth day he sent the people away; and they blessed the king, and went to their tents joyful and glad of heart for all the good that the Lord had done for His servant David, and for Israel His people.*

With that scripture in mind, imagine the Rapture just happening. "All" God's people are gathered with Him in heaven—a "great assembly." We are gathered for a "feast"—the Marriage Supper of the Lamb, "before the Lord our God." When the feast or Marriage Supper is over, the celebration will continue in heaven as the Lord sends us to our "tents" or the places the Lord has prepared for us. We are praising and "blessing the King" being "joyful and glad of heart" for all the Lord has done for us. The imagery and wording of this Scripture appear to be a foreshadowing of what we may participate in when we enter heaven.

When we get to heaven at the Rapture, Christ's spiritual temple—His Church, will be complete. There will be a great celebration and feast just as it was when Solomon's temple was completed. Solomon's celebration lasted fourteen days and the days were divided into two sections of seven days. At this point he separated the people on the eighth day, which was actually the eighth day following the second set of seven days—the fifteenth day. From the seventy week prophecy of Daniel, we already know for that time one day represented one year. If this particular scripture has significance for a future event, then it certainly could be that the fourteen days of Solomon's celebration could equate to a fourteen year celebration in heaven after the Rapture. You can see that the people are gathered for a period of seven days or symbolic seven years, which could be seven years before the Tribulation begins. The second set of seven days, or future seven years could very well be the time of the Tribulation. The fifteenth day, or the first day after the celebration, could symbolize the beginning of the first year of Christ's millennial kingdom on the earth.

1 Kings 8 verse 66 is the very last verse of the chapter and then chapter nine opens with what could be seen symbolically as a significant event. Most Bibles have a caption at the start of chapter nine to summarize what the chapter is about. The caption or summary given for chapter nine is "God's second appearance to Solomon." God's second appearance to Solomon seems to have similarities to Christ's second coming. The way this Scripture is laid out in the Bible shows a celebration divided into two, seven day or future year segments totaling fourteen days or years. This is followed by a second appearance of God to Solomon, or a symbolic second coming of Christ.

If God is revealing to us in Scripture a foreshadowing of a future time based on these past events surrounding the completion of the first temple and all the symbolism that encompasses, then this is something to get excited about. This may point to the Rapture occurring sooner than later in these last days, especially if you consider when the Tribulation may begin.

You can dive even deeper into the analysis of this interpretation of Scripture. This same story in 1 Kings is also retold with a different perspective and detail in 2 Chronicles. When Christ returns at the end of the Tribulation He is coming to the earth to dwell with His people and be their King. He will be worshipped and praised for His goodness. After Solomon built the temple, God showed up and the people responded.

> *2 Chronicles 7:1-3 1 When Solomon had finished praying, fire came down from heaven and consumed the burnt offering and the sacrifices; and the glory of the Lord filled the temple. 2 And*

> the priests could not enter the house of the Lord, because the glory of the Lord had filled the Lord's house. 3 When all the children of Israel saw how the fire came down, and the glory of the Lord on the temple, they bowed their faces to the ground on the pavement, and worshiped and praised the Lord, saying: "For He is good, For His mercy endures forever."

In like manner, when Christ returns the remnant of Israel will respond to Him.

> Zechariah 12:10 "And I will pour on the house of David and on the inhabitants of Jerusalem the Spirit of grace and supplication; then they will look on Me whom they pierced. Yes, they will mourn for Him as one mourns for his only son, and grieve for Him as one grieves for a firstborn.

At Christ's return, He will pour out His Spirit on Israel and they will recognize their guilt for rejecting their Messiah, but He will be there in Person to restore that broken relationship. He will be their God just as He has promised. What they were looking for and missed at the time of Christ's first coming, they will have now found at His second coming. The foreshadowing associated with God coming down in fire and filling the temple to be with His people, will be fulfilled completely as Christ begins His millennial reign on the earth. The severed connection and relationship with Israel will be fully restored.

> 2 Chronicles 7:8-11 8 At that time Solomon kept the feast seven days, and all Israel with him, a very great assembly from the entrance of Hamath to the Brook of Egypt. 9 And on the eighth day they held a sacred assembly, for they observed the dedication of the alter seven days, and the feast seven days. 10 On the twenty-third day of the seventh month he sent the people away to their tents, joyful and glad of heart for the good that the Lord had done for David, for Solomon, and for His people Israel. 11 Thus Solomon finished the house of the Lord and the king's house; and Solomon successfully accomplished all that came into his heart to make in the house of the Lord and in his own house.

The feast that Israel celebrated was the Feast of Tabernacles, which began on the fifteenth day of the seventh month (Tishri) and lasted through the twenty-second day. Seven days prior began the dedication of the altar, which started on the eighth of Tishri, 958 B.C. The first temple served as the center for Israel's national and spiritual life for about 400 years, until it was destroyed by the Babylonians in 586 B.C.

The Feast of Tabernacles is prophetically relevant in regards to Christ's millennial kingdom, as well as the fact that it was celebrated at the dedication of the temple. In Hebrew, the Feast of Tabernacles is called Sukkot (pronounced Soo-Cote). The festival is in commemoration of God providing for the children of Israel as they wandered in the desert for forty years. Sukkot is a time for Israel to renew fellowship with the Lord as they honor Him for all He has done for them. It is one of three feasts commanded by the Lord to be celebrated by Israel (*Deuteronomy 16:13*). They celebrate Sukkot in the fall at harvest time during the months of September or October. The holiday also became known as the "Feast of Ingathering" and the "Feast of Booths." In ancient Israel it was such a significant and joyous holiday that it became simply known as "The Feast."

"The Feast" was celebrated at the dedication of the temple as the presence of God came to dwell with His people. We now have access to the heavenly temple of God through Christ our mediator and intercessor. We the Church, are the temple of His body and are anticipating the celebration we will partake in when this temple is complete at the Rapture.

Israel's future hope anticipates when Christ brings His kingdom to this earth. All the nations who survive the Tribulation will gather together yearly to worship the Lord together in Jerusalem during the Feast of Tabernacles.

> *And it shall come to pass that everyone who is left of all the nations which came against Jerusalem shall go up from year to year to worship the King, the Lord of hosts, and to keep the Feast of Tabernacles (Zechariah 14:16).*

Jesus came to this world to redeem its people from sin through His death and resurrection. Here He "tabernacled among us." The earth and all creation are now groaning for that day when restoration is complete, and Christ is once again "tabernacling" or dwelling on the earth with His people.

And the Word became flesh and dwelt (tabernacled) *among us, and we beheld His glory, the glory as of the only begotten of the Father, full of grace and truth (John 1:14).*

Part Three—Section 8

So, here's where putting all the "biblical" pieces of the puzzle together begins to get exciting as the day we are now living in rapidly approaches a new era. There has been no other day in history as significant prophetically since the day of Pentecost as May 14, 1948—the rebirth of the nation of Israel. Prior to the Balfour Declaration of 1917 resulting in the Jews migrating back to their homeland, there were no real signs on the earth that we were living in the last days of this era or approaching the times of the end. Since then, Israel blossomed and that day marked the beginning of the "generation" that would be alive to see the return of Christ.

Technology has increased to where we can easily conceive of the unbelievable events as spoken of in the book of Revelation actually taking place. Before, the thoughts of those events were unimaginable. The world stage has been set and people's minds have been rewired to think that a one world government is a good idea. The deception needed for the Antichrist to rise is deeply ingrained in the hearts and minds of the unredeemed. Their hearts have become hardened to truth.

Large parts of the Church of Jesus Christ have fallen into great apostasy in recent years as prophesied would happen in the last days. Many denominations, pastors, and false converts have come to the errant conclusion that the Bible is not fully God's Word, that it's acceptable to murder babies, or for people and even pastors to live sexually deviant lifestyles. False doctrines teaching many ways to get to heaven besides Christ, that there is no hell or devil, or that the main meaning of the Bible is to help the poor have crept into the pulpits. This is eternally destroying countless souls. There has never been a greater separation in what is called Christianity, but Christ's true followers (the remnant of Christianity) are beginning to rise for His glory in these last days. Millions are accepting the truth of the gospel and are seeing the hand of God move in powerful ways as He is preparing them for an eternity with Him.

The words that Jesus spoke to His disciples on the Mount of Olives are coming to life daily as we read them in the headlines, or watch in disbelief on the TV screen. Natural disaster, wars, famines, plagues, pestilence, violence, hatred, apostasy, idolatry, and deception are all increasing exponentially in frequency and magnitude just as the Bible said it would prior to the Lord's return and the end of this age. To what level of depravity has humanity fallen to, when the most dangerous and deadly place on the planet is inside a mother's womb? Is there any question that it is high-time for God to judge this world and purge it from its filth? Let this warning from Jesus be a reminder to us all.

Matthew 24:37-39 37 But as the days of Noah were, so also will be the coming of the Son of Man be. 38 For as in the days before the flood, they were eating and drinking, marrying and giving in marriage, until the day that Noah entered the ark, 39 and did not know until the flood came and took them all away, so also will the coming of the Son of Man be.

Part Three—Section 9

Consider what the near future may look like for you if Christ's timing for the completion of His Church and the nation Israel falls along a similar time table as it has in the past. Biblical history shows us patterns the Lord has used before in redeeming Israel. Will He stay consistent with what He has previously done as the redemption plan of our day unfolds? Day one of the "generation that will not pass away" began on May 14, 1948. The fig tree parable from *Matthew 24* points to the rise of Israel as the event that marks the beginning of that generation. According to Scripture, the time allotted for the lifespan of a generation does not appear to exceed eighty years. Eighty years throughout Scripture appears to be a time period the Lord has used in past dealings with redeeming Israel, especially their redemption from Egypt through Moses.

God has always been consistent in dealing with His children for many reasons; one being so that we can trust Him and know that what He says and does is true and good. Christ said that He would someday return in judgment, and He will. He said He would fulfill His promises to Israel, and He will. He said He would spare His Church from the wrath to come, and He will. IF God chooses to be consistent with His use of an eighty year redemption plan for Israel, and IF the generation Jesus spoke about began in 1948, THEN there is a high likelihood that Christ could return and establish His millennial reign in the year 2028. IF that happens, THEN the Tribulation will begin in the year 2021.

In understanding what we have learned about the timing of the Rapture, we know that the Church will be removed from the world before the Tribulation begins. It is logical to assume that there will need to be a significant time span between these two events. The Antichrist will need to rise to power and establish his kingdom and America needs to fall from world domination. Neither of those events will happen overnight. The Lord loves the number seven—His perfect number. It is also logical for Him to use a time span of seven years prior to the seven year Tribulation as a time for His Church to participate in heavenly activities before judgment is focused upon the earth.

When Solomon finished building the Lord's temple, a symbolic version of heaven—God's dwelling place, he had a celebration with the people in the presence of God that lasted fourteen days. If that event has any symbolic foreshadowing of the kind of celebration we will experience in heaven, then our celebration after the Rapture could comparatively last fourteen years. If that is the case, the bottom line is that there is the possibility, Lord willing, Christ would return to earth in 2028, the Tribulation would begin in 2021, and the Rapture could occur in the year 2014. Christian, if this possible scenario does not get you excited then what will? Our time left here could be very short.

Don't be bothered if you are by hearing specific years being mentioned for the Lord's return. Jesus said that no one would know the day or hour of His return. It would be foolish and impossible to claim to know what day our Lord will return at the Rapture. It would be foolish to state with certainty the year this will happen as well. This is not an attempt to do either. The Lord has left clues and prophecies in the Scripture regarding the end times that are being fulfilled daily. He has also given us His Spirit and a sound mind to be able to contemplate and think on His ways. In understanding the ways of God revealed to us in His Word, He expects us to critically examine His Word and to desire to know Him and His plans for us to the fullest extent.

It is a fact that the Lord will physically return to the earth and there will be a specific number of years that pass between the rebirth of Israel in 1948 and that Day. In studying Scripture and modern and historical events, it appears the Bible may be revealing a possible amount of years for that time period. God can and will do what He desires as He completes His perfect sovereign and providential will for mankind and all creation on His timetable. With that in mind, there can only be positive effects on the life of the Christian who thinks about and anticipates with an earnest desire, the return of the Lord for His Bride and all the future glory that entails.

The Lord has promised a great eternal reward—the crown of righteousness, to those who love and look forward to His coming.

Finally, there is laid up for me the crown of righteousness, which the Lord, the righteous Judge, will give to me on that Day, and not to me only but also to all who have loved His appearing (2 Timothy 4:8).

What you don't want to be is a mocker, and scoff at His coming. If you have the attitude that it just doesn't matter when the Lord returns; "He'll come when He wants to." and could care less—do you really believe He is coming back at all? If you have this mindset, you are actually fulfilling a biblical end times' prophecy and proving that His return is near. Consider this Scripture:

2 Peter 3:3-4 3 knowing this first: that scoffers will come in the last days, walking according to their own lusts, 4 and saying, "Where is the promise of His coming? For since the fathers fell asleep, all things continue as they were from the beginning of creation."

Other than your salvation, what can be more relevant and important in the days we are living than the Lord's return and imminent Rapture of His Church? 2014 may come and go like any of the other recent years we have experienced with world events and turmoil continuing on a downhill spiral. If January 1, 2015 rolls around and you're still here, your heart and eyes should definitely be fixed on the Lord and the skies. This should only be a source of encouragement showing that we are yet one year closer to the Lord's imminent return.

As you contemplate the possibility of a 2014 Rapture, think about this. Again, the only significance this may have is if it actually happens this way. How many years are there between 1948 and 2014. Answer—66. What importance, if any, does the number 66 have biblically?

There are 66 books written in the Bible. The 66th book of the Bible is the Revelation of Jesus Christ. The book of Isaiah is often referred to as the gospel of the Old Testament. It explains salvation through Christ and prophetically references Jesus more than any other Old Testament book. There are 66 chapters in the book of Isaiah. Isaiah chapter 66 is one of the strongest Messianic chapters regarding Christ's second coming. It also prophesies the rebirth of Israel in 1948 (vs. 8). The number six in the Bible is known to be the number of man. God created man on the sixth day of creation. In the book of Revelation you see the number 666 as an unholy number that the Antichrist uses to mark his followers, known as the mark of the beast. Though that number is unholy, there is nothing unholy about 66. Christ returning for His Church 66 years after Israel's rebirth could be another one of those significant numbers that God uses to fulfill that time span. This is just an interesting idea to contemplate, nothing more. If the year 2014 comes and goes with no Rapture, then this idea has absolutely no relevance. Who can fathom the mind and plans of God? Just be excited He has a plan that includes you!

Part Three—Section 10

If you are a bit skeptical or uncertain of what you think the Bible is saying about the Rapture, you may feel more comfortable with the idea after examining the most descriptive and specific Rapture event in the Bible that we have to compare our future Rapture to. Elijah's Rapture, when he was taken to heaven in a chariot of fire, is by far the Bible's most well-known Rapture story we can explore and learn from in comparison to our own future Rapture experience.

You may not remember or have even realized before, but Elijah, Elisha, and many people and prophets in their region at that time knew beforehand that Elijah was going to be taken away by God. They even knew the exact day he would leave. We learn about this story in the book of 2 Kings. The only thing it appears they did not know was at what hour of that day it would happen and in what manner he would be taken. The Bible does not state how this information became known to them, but there must have been a divine revelation in some fashion to reveal that Elijah would be raptured. That information then spread across the region. It was an expected event that was imminent on the very day he left. Follow along with this story. It is quite amazing!

> *2 Kings 2:1-12 1 And it came to pass, when the Lord was about to take up Elijah into heaven by a whirlwind, that Elijah went with Elisha from Gilgal. 2 Then Elijah said to Elisha, "Stay here, please, for the Lord has sent me on to Bethel." But Elisha said, "As the Lord lives, and as your soul lives, I will not leave you!" So they went down to Bethel. 3 Now the sons of the prophets who were at Bethel came out to Elisha, and said to him, "Do you know that the Lord will take away your master from over you today?" And he said, "Yes, I know; keep silent!" 4 Then Elijah said to him, "Elisha, stay here, please, for the Lord has sent me on to Jericho." But he said, "As the Lord lives and as your soul lives, I will not leave you!" So they came to Jericho. 5 Now the sons of the prophets who were at Jericho came to Elisha and said to him, "Do*

you know that the Lord will take away your master from over you today?" So he answered, "Yes, I know; keep silent!" 6 Then Elijah said to him, "Stay here, please, for the Lord has sent me on to the Jordan." But he said, "As the Lord lives, and as your soul lives, I will not leave you!" So the two of them went on. 7 And fifty men of the sons of the prophets went and stood facing them at a distance, while the two of them stood by the Jordan. 8 Now Elijah took his mantle, rolled it up, and struck the water; and it was divided this way and that, so that the two of them crossed over on dry ground. 9 And so it was, when they had crossed over, that Elijah said to Elisha, "Ask! What may I do for you, before I am taken away from you?" Elisha said, "Please let a double portion of your spirit be upon me." 10 So he said, "You have asked a hard thing. Nevertheless, if you see me when I am taken from you, it shall be so for you; but if not, it shall not be so." 11 Then it happened, as they continued on and talked, that suddenly a chariot of fire appeared with horses of fire, and separated the two of them; and Elijah went up by a whirlwind into heaven. 12 And Elisha saw it, and he cried out, "My father, my father, the chariot of Israel and its horsemen!" So he saw him no more. And he took hold of his own clothes and tore them into two pieces.

Notice that as they travelled from town to town that Elisha refused to leave Elijah knowing Elijah was about to leave. The people kept pestering Elisha with the information that Elijah was leaving him that very day and it bothered Elisha. Elisha did not want his mentor and friend to leave him. As they supernaturally crossed the Jordan River, they had now drawn a crowd who were watching expectantly to watch Elijah leave. Elijah knew he was about to be taken, but did not know all the details of his departure. He even wondered if Elisha would see him leave.

Elijah was prompted by the Holy Spirit to offer Elisha a great gift, but he did not know if what Elisha asked for was even possible. Indeed it turns out it was. Elisha did receive the same ministry that Elijah had and carried on the workings of the power of the Holy Spirit with great signs and miracles up to the day of his death. In fact, there are more documented miracles in the Bible that Elisha performed by God than Elijah did.

There is great similarity with the way Jesus ascended into heaven as He left his disciples after His resurrection as to Elijah's ascension. After Jesus went to heaven, His Spirit and power were given to His Church on the day of Pentecost just as God's Spirit and power passed from Elijah to Elisha. Elijah appears to have been raptured by the Holy Spirit. The wind and fire that were involved are both symbolic representations of the Holy Spirit in the Bible. Our Rapture will be caused by Jesus Christ, as it is He who we meet in the clouds as we ascend. Elijah and the people of his day knew close to the exact time his Rapture would happen; they just did not know in what manner it would happen.

Part Three—Section 11

We as followers of Christ know the details of how our Rapture and departure will occur; we just do not know the day or hour it will happen. Just as Elijah and Elisha were walking and talking and Elijah was suddenly taken, our Rapture occurs in a similar way. We will be walking, talking, working, playing, sleeping, and carrying on with normal daily life, when instantly in the blink of an eye our existence will change drastically. We will be changed, transformed in a flash, and ushered into the clouds where we will meet Jesus Christ and He will take us to heaven.

Our Rapture is different and unique from other biblical raptures in that it occurs the same time the Resurrection happens. All believers in Christ who have died will be physically reunited with their dead bodies. They will be resurrected to life into an eternal, new, imperishable body just as our bodies will be transformed into at that same time as we then all go to meet Jesus. Is there anything you can think about or contemplate at this point in our lives more exciting and anticipated than that? It is the next major event all of heaven is waiting for and bursting at the seams to experience. Heaven is about to explode with joy as a reunion and celebration never seen before is about to take place.

We on earth are often so closed minded and short sighted about our thoughts towards the Rapture and being taken to heaven. We often don't realize the magnitude of the event in understanding that this is the *Resurrection*, of which Jesus Christ was the first fruits. Those in heaven now are not waiting for Christ to return to earth at the end of the Tribulation, though they understand they will participate in that and it too will be a glorious day for them. The day they are now waiting eagerly for is the Resurrection and Rapture of the Church of Jesus Christ. This day involves them just as much as it does us. How long will the Lord tarry in His coming for us?

Do not take a gamble with thinking you have more time here than you really have. Christ could take you today in death, He could take you today in the Rapture, or you could be left behind. What you believe or are led to believe regarding Jesus and His plans for humanity does not change the reality of what will happen. Jesus will not come back at the roll of a dice. He is not sitting in heaven drawing straws for the day He takes action. Jesus and Satan are not gathered together somewhere playing rock, paper, scissors to see who makes the next move or who wins. The day of the Resurrection and every day of existence, including every day of your life, has been strategically planned and laid out. For God, it's as if every day has already happened from eternity past, before the earth, creation, or time ever existed. God's plans have no beginning, they have always been. God is in control and He always wins in the end!

Part Three—Section 12

Here's What the Apostle Paul Has to Say About the Rapture

1 Thessalonians 4:13-18 13 But I do not want you to be ignorant, brethren, concerning those who have fallen asleep, lest you sorrow as others who have no hope. 14 For if we believe that Jesus died and rose again, even so God will bring with Him those who sleep in Jesus. 15 For this we say to you by the word of the Lord, that we who are alive and remain until the coming of the Lord will by no means precede those who are asleep. 16 For the Lord Himself will descend from heaven with a shout, with the voice of an archangel, and with the trumpet of God. And the dead in Christ will rise first. 17 Then we who are alive and remain shall be caught up together with them in the clouds to meet the Lord in the air. And thus we shall always be with the Lord. 18 Therefore comfort one another with these words.

1 Corinthians 15:50-55 50 Now this I say, brethren, that flesh and blood cannot inherit the kingdom of God; nor does corruption inherit incorruption. 51 Behold, I tell you a mystery: We shall not all sleep, but we shall all be changed—52 in a moment, in the twinkling of an eye, at the last trumpet. For the trumpet will sound, and the dead will be raised incorruptible, and we shall be changed. 53 For this corruptible must put on incorruption, and this mortal must put on immortality. 54 So when this corruptible has put on incorruption, and this mortal has put on immortality, then shall be brought to pass the saying that is written: "Death is swallowed up in victory." 55 "O Death, where is your sting? O Hades, where is your victory?"

Philippians 3:20-21 20 For our citizenship is in heaven, from which we also eagerly wait for the Savior, the Lord Jesus Christ,

21 who will transform our lowly body that it may be conformed to His glorious body, according to the working by which He is able even to subdue all things to Himself.

1 John 3:2 (written by John) *Beloved, now we are children of God; and it has not yet been revealed what we shall be, but we know that when He is revealed, we shall be like Him, for we shall see Him as He is.*

Colossians 3:4 When Christ who is our life appears, then you also will appear with Him in glory.

1 Thessalonians 5:9-10 9 For God did not appoint us to wrath, but to obtain salvation through our Lord Jesus Christ, 10 who died for us, that whether we wake or sleep, we should live together with Him.

1 Thessalonians 1:10 …and to wait for His Son from heaven, whom He raised from the dead, even Jesus who delivers us from the wrath to come.

Titus 2:11-14 11 For the grace of God that brings salvation has appeared to all men, 12 teaching us that, denying ungodliness and worldly lusts, we should live soberly, righteously, and godly in the present age, 13 looking for the blessed hope and glorious appearing of our great God and Savior Jesus Christ, 14 who gave Himself for us, that He might redeem us from every lawless deed and purify for Himself His own special people, zealous for good works.

Here's What the Lord Jesus Christ Has to Say About the Rapture

John 14:1-3 1 "Let not your heart be troubled; you believe in God, believe also in Me. 2 In My Father's house are many mansions; if it were not so, I would have told you. I go to prepare a place for you. 3 And if I go and prepare a place for you, I will come again and receive you to Myself; that where I am, there you may be also. 4 And where I go you know, and the way you know."

Luke 21:34-36 34 "But take heed to yourselves, lest your hearts be weighed down with carousing, drunkenness, and cares of this life, and that Day come on you unexpectedly. 35 For it will come as a snare on all those who dwell on the face of the whole earth. 36 Watch therefore, and pray always that you may be counted worthy to escape all these things that will come to pass, and to stand before the Son of Man."

Revelation 3:10 Because you have kept My command to persevere, I also will keep you from the hour of trial which shall come upon the whole world, to test those who dwell on the earth.

Revelation 22:12 "And behold, I am coming quickly, and My reward is with Me, to give to every one according to his work.

Part Three—Section 13

If you claim to be and are a follower of the Lord Jesus Christ, you might be asking yourself or God, "How can I possibly prepare for the day of the Rapture?" "What should I be doing if these truly are the last days of life as we know it?" Besides the obvious answer of reading the Bible, praying, and gathering with other believers; follow some advice that Joshua gave the children of Israel regarding how they should respond to God in the days they were living in. The advice is timeless and is as relevant today as in any other time in history.

The main point of *Joshua 22:5* is: *to love the Lord your God, to walk in all His ways, to keep His commandments, to hold fast to Him, and to serve Him with all your heart and with all your soul.* If you live your life by these guidelines, as Joshua laid out in God's Word, then you will be prepared for the day of the Rapture, you will not fail, and will be found worthy at the judgment. Your reward will truly be great.

If you have rejected Christ so far in this life or claim to be associated with Christianity, but have no personal relationship with the Lord Jesus Christ, then your response to being enlightened by and exposed to the Word of God needs to be different in these last days. You cannot simply expect to fall under the protection of God, or expect to be Raptured from the time of the Tribulation that is coming just because you think you are a good person, or think that God in some way feels you have earned enough points. If you think you deserve to be saved based on good things you've accomplished in this life, you are wrong and have been deceived by the father of lies—Satan.

What you think you may know about God does not change the facts or reality of who He is and how He says He will deal with you according to His Word. It is true that God loves you deeply and desires passionately that you not perish. He yearns that you respond to His Word according to His ways and not your own. If you refuse or reject God's ways, then you make yourself an enemy of God and a child of Satan. That is what God's Word says about the condition you are in.

The result of that condition is to be eternally separated from God in a place that has been prepared for Satan and his unholy angels.

The path to God is easily understood, but not easy. The mind of a child can comprehend the grace and mercy that He offers to each one of us, but the road to get there is narrow, difficult, and impossible to attain without the guidance and direction of the Holy Spirit. There is nothing you can do in God's eyes to make yourself a good person, or to make God love you any more than He already does. There is no such thing as a good person. The Bible says that all have sinned and have fallen short of God's glory and that there is no one that does good. What is God's glory? God's glory is sinless perfection just as He is. This is an unattainable pursuit that no human ever born since Adam and Eve is possible of achieving; accept for our Lord Jesus Christ.

Where God lives, no corrupt or sinful thing can ever dwell. Once sin entered humanity, it cursed the entire gene pool and all have been condemned. That sounds very depressing and unfair when you look at it from outside of God's plans, but that is where it gets interesting. In understanding God's plans for redeeming humanity from sin, is where what He has done for us gets exciting! God offers us all a way and a plan to receive forgiveness and redemption, and to be cleansed from the filth that plagues each one of us. Instead of being a child of the devil, we can be called children of God, saints, and heirs to His kingdom. Isn't it absolutely wonderful that He has provided a way, not many ways—ONE WAY—to be saved from His justice? How simple it is to be able to only have to understand just one way to get to heaven and have eternal life.

His plan for us has proven to all of creation that He is a God of sacrificial love, kindness, and compassion, full of grace, mercy, and truth. If you are unaware of what God's plan to save you is all about, then you and you alone need to make the decision to ask God to reveal that plan to you. If you have ever prayed to God under the condition you are now in, He has never heard or acknowledged your prayers. Sadly, you are not His child or a part of His kingdom. Your sin has separated you from your Creator. The first prayer that He will hear and acknowledge from you is that first prayer to God where you ask God to show Himself to you, to forgive you, and to save you. A prayer like that gets God's attention and He is more than willing and able to oblige.

God has given humanity, especially in the modern days we are living in, His Word—The Bible. The Bible is not just a book, but a living, breathing receptacle; a way to plug in directly to the mind and heart of God. The way God has established communication with humanity during this age we are now in is through His written Word. The Bible is difficult, if not impossible to comprehend without God's guidance. God's Holy Spirit will work in your life if you choose to humble yourself and allow Him to take control of your life as you pursue knowledge of God through His Word. At that point, it is as if scales that are clouding your vision will be removed from your eyes. His Word will become alive in your life as God talks to you through His Word and makes Himself known in a powerful way. It is unavoidable.

If the burden of sin is weighing heavily on your soul, and you feel you are being drawn towards God and are wanting to receive forgiveness, salvation, and establish a relationship with your Creator—the Lord Jesus Christ, do not deny this burden. This is the calling of God on your life.

There are three important questions that you will need to find answers to and accept as truth if you choose. The answers to these questions hold the power of eternal life. The answers can be found in the Bible through the direction and guidance of the Holy Spirit. The three questions are:

1) Who is Jesus Christ?

2) What has Jesus Christ done for me?

3) How should I respond to what Jesus Christ has done for me?

Here is a list of some scriptures from the Bible that will guide you as you seek to learn more about God. Eternal life is a free gift that you can either choose to receive or reject. Grab hold of a Bible—God's Word, and dive into these Scriptures as you find The Answer to life.

Scriptures About What Jesus Christ Has Done for You

Romans 3:23, Romans 6:23, Isaiah 53:6, Hebrews 9:27, Romans 5:8-10, John 14:6, Revelation 3:20, Acts 4:12, John 3:16-21, Acts 2:38, Romans 10:13, 1 John 1:9, Ephesians 2:8-9, 2 Corinthians 5:17, Romans 10:9-10, John 1:12, 1 Peter 3:18, Mark 1:15, Acts 16:31, Mark 16:16, Psalm 103:12, Isaiah 9:6, Matthew 1:21, Hebrews 1:3, Philippians 2:9-11, Colossians 1:15-22, John 1:1-18, John 10:30, John 14:8-10, Romans 8:9-11, Matthew 28:20, Revelation 3:21, Revelation 22:12-13,16, 1 Corinthians 15:1-28.

Part Four

Where Have They Gone?

An Explanation for Those Not Taken When the People Vanished

Section 1

During the last days of this era, an event is going to occur across the world that will shake the core beliefs of everyone on the planet. This event will be so mind blowing, catastrophic, and confusing that most won't want to talk about it, think about it, or accept it as truth. For many who have doubted the existence of God, those doubts will cease. Others' doubts will increase. There will now be possible proof of the existence of aliens, or an encounter of some kind with an intelligent being or beings that have powers and capabilities greater than our own. Fear of the unknown will grip the heart of mankind.

When it happens, many will remember a friend, relative, book, movie, or article that mentioned or talked about this very thing happening, but they just shrugged it off as superstition, a fairy tale, or flat out disbelief. Now it has happened and it's too late. If you are reading this and it hasn't happened yet, you may not know what this is all about. If it has happened, you know full well and wish it hadn't, hoping that what you saw take place before your very eyes was at best a bad dream. In reality, it has become the world's worst nightmare. As bad as this is, it is only the beginning of the nightmare about to be unleashed on the world.

In an instant, a moment, a flash in time, mass populations of people across the globe will have vanished. The people disappeared into thin air and they did this in front of the world, as the world watched in disbelief. As strangely as they vanished, even more perplexing is what these people left behind. Clothes, eye glasses, contact lens', wigs, dentures, dental fillings, jewelry, pace-makers, prosthetics—anything that was attached to, in, or draped on their physical bodies did not disappear, but were left in a heap on the ground or blowing away in the wind.

The disappearance was caught on live camera, video, and photographs from every part of the planet. Some people disappeared in the quiet of their home and maybe no one saw them go. Others were witnessed leaving by many, possibly thousands, or millions depending on circumstances. Automobiles, planes, boats, and trains being driven by people who vanished, were left unmanned and crashed violently, came to a stop peacefully, or fell forcefully from the sky all over the world. People doing very important things left at very inopportune times, such as doctors doing critical procedures, firefighters rescuing the helpless, pilots flying large passenger planes, or world leaders conducting the affairs of man. At first, the disappearances seemed to be random; a mix from all walks of life, but upon close examination of who went a similar bond was found to exist. In all, an estimation or conservative guess of 400 million to one billion people vanished at the same time—people from all ages and all locations.

If you were witness to this event, it is likely you have already formed an opinion as to what occurred. You either think you know, don't know, or don't care to know what caused millions to vanish in an instant. What many may be thinking is that aliens or beings from another world were involved and responsible for the disappearance. This will likely be one of two, or three of the most common explanations.

Another view may be that these people had evolved into a higher state of being, transcended the physical realm and entered into a metaphysical realm, or other dimension. There will be no evidence to back up either of these theories. The truth behind what happened is that God—the Lord Jesus Christ, removed His followers and children from the earth in an event that Christians have come to call the "Rapture."

Chances are you have heard the term "Rapture" before, but did not know or understand what it was all about. Maybe you knew all about the Rapture and just flat out rejected the idea. You now know and have seen it firsthand. The Bible—God's Word, has revealed that this exact day would happen. It has been no secret in these last days. Christians for centuries have been discussing it, anticipating it, and telling others that it could happen at any time. In recent years, there have been many popular books such as the "Left Behind" series, movies, and coverage and discussion of this event in the different media forums.

You may feel lucky that you weren't taken and are sorry for those that were. If that is what you think, you are deceived. It is you who should be pitied. Not only is this proof that you are not one of God's children and are headed for an eternity separated from God, but according to the Bible, you have been left to live in the most troubling and destructive time in earth's history. The true Christians of the world, those who have chosen to serve Jesus Christ as Lord of their life, have been rescued from the wrath of God about to be poured out on mankind and upon the earth.

As bad as that sounds, if you are interested there is still a chance for redemption from God to be granted to you during this time. Followers of Jesus Christ who were taken are now in heaven with Him. Don't give up hope. The path has been paved for you to receive forgiveness for your rejection of Jesus Christ and to one day enter into heaven and participate in God's eternal plans for your life, if you so desire. This is not the time to be a skeptic, but a believer in God—the Lord Jesus Christ.

During your life you have probably heard the saying, "someday Jesus is coming back." The Rapture is part of Jesus coming back. He came back and met His Church—the Christians, in the clouds and then took them to heaven (*1 Thessalonians 4:13-18*). There is a time in the near future though, when Jesus will come back to the earth to physically appear to everyone and rule the planet as King. When He comes back the second time, if you are not one of His followers, then you will be considered His enemy. You will be cast from the earth into eternal torment based on your choice to reject the Savior. The choice is yours!

Part Four—Section 2

If you are unsure why Jesus Christ removed His followers from the world and don't understand what He is protecting them from; here is the answer. In the near future, a time period of seven years of judgment called the Tribulation will begin. During this time, God removes His restraint of protection on the world and judges the people of the world for their sin and rebellion against Him. He literally pours out His wrath on the unredeemed. This time of judgment is so severe, the Bible says that if God did not put an end to it, no one on the planet would survive it. That's why it only lasts seven years. At the end of the seven year Tribulation period, Jesus Christ returns to establish His earthly rule as King of Kings and Lord of Lords. His justice will endure forever. If you can manage to survive the time of the Tribulation, you will be witness to the Lord's second coming—His glorious and triumphant appearing.

The Bible reveals that during the first three and a half years of the Tribulation, half the world's population will be killed in the horrific catastrophes, wars, and disasters that come upon the earth. During the second half of the Tribulation, known as the Great Tribulation, things get even worse. During this time, two-thirds of the Jews on the planet are killed *(Zechariah 13:8-9)*. It is likely that seventy-five percent or more of the world's population will be dead at the end of the Tribulation when Christ returns. The horror will be unspeakable. The Bible declares that it is the worst time of trouble, judgment, and disaster that has ever been, or will be on the face of the earth *(Daniel 12:1)*. When He does return, those who are not His followers—all who have rejected and rebelled against Him, are separated and destroyed. Those who are left are only a small remnant or minority of the earth's previous population, but will be received by their King to participate in His new kingdom of perfect justice and peace. Whose side will you choose to be on?

In the Bible, the book of Revelation—a book about future prophetic events, declares very specifically the type of judgments that will come and in what order they fall. It is not all doom and gloom. The end of the book reveals the glory of God and His plans to bring peace to the earth as He makes all things new and perfect according to His will.

This is what the book of Revelation says happens to the earth and those dwelling on it during the time of the Tribulation. The book of Revelation reveals in chronological order the horror that will unfold during the Tribulation into three categories: the *Seal Judgments*, the *Trumpet Judgments*, and the *Bowl Judgments*. Each judgment is broken down into seven events that take place. Let's examine these judgments and see what will occur, or may be occurring while you are reading this.

Seal Judgments: *(Revelation 6 and 8:1-6)*

- *1st Seal*—The Antichrist sets out to conquer the world.

- *2nd Seal*—War breaks out across the globe and there is no peace.

- *3rd Seal*—Extreme economic collapse world-wide, famine, and loss of material wealth.

- *4th Seal*—Widespread death on the earth from starvation, war, and calamity. One fourth of the world's population dies.

- *5th Seal*—Extreme martyrdom and persecution for believing in Christ.

- *6th Seal*—A great earthquake happens followed by terrifying signs in the heavens. The sun goes dark, the moon turns red, and stars or possibly meteors fall to the earth. The earth's atmosphere becomes disturbed and mountains and islands all over the earth are moved out of place.

- *7th Seal*—The initiation of the first of the trumpet judgments. There is silence in heaven for thirty minutes. Seven angels are given seven trumpets as the judgments are prepared to be unleashed. Fire is thrown from heaven to earth.

Trumpet Judgments: *(Revelation 8:7-13 and 9 and 11:15-19)*

- *1st Trumpet*—Hail and fire fall to the earth and destroy one third of the earth's trees and vegetation.

- *2nd Trumpet*—Something like a great mountain burning with fire is thrown into the sea. A third of the sea turns to blood, a third of the seas living creatures die, and a third of the seas ships are destroyed.

- *3rd Trumpet*—A star called Wormwood falls from the sky burning like a torch and poisons a third of the world's rivers and springs causing many to die who drink from the water.

- *4th Trumpet*—A catastrophe happens that darkens the sun, moon, and stars. A third of a day does not shine.

- *5th Trumpet*—Demonic creatures something like scorpions and locust are loosed from hell to attack men and sting them, but will not kill them. The creatures will be ruled by the angel from the bottomless pit. The pain will be so severe men will want to die, but won't be able to. They torment people for five months.

- *6th Trumpet*—Four of the most evil demons in existence who had been bound are released. They kill one third of mankind. They may do this supernaturally or use war.

- *7th Trumpet*—Prelude to the bowl judgments. The kingdom of Christ is proclaimed in heaven accompanied by great worship. On earth there are lightnings, noises, thunderings, an earthquake, and great hail.

Bowl Judgments: *(Revelation 16)*

- *1st Bowl*—Foul and loathsome sores come upon those who worship the Antichrist.

- *2nd Bowl*—All of the sea turns to blood, killing all creatures of the sea.

- *3rd Bowl*—All of the rivers and springs turn to blood.

- **4th Bowl**—Extreme heat from the sun scorches men with fire who blaspheme God and refuse to repent.
- **5th Bowl**—The Antichrist's kingdom becomes dark and intense pain comes upon his followers. They blaspheme God because of their sores and pain.
- **6th Bowl**—The Euphrates River dries up and three demons go out to create war in the valley of Armageddon. The dried up river will allow a 200 million man army from Asia to cross and come to Israel for battle.
- **7th Bowl**—A loud voice from the temple of heaven declares, "It is done!" The largest earthquake in history occurs and the city of Jerusalem is divided into three parts. The quake causes all islands to disappear and the mountains to crumble, changing earth's topography. Then 100 pound hail stones fall from the sky upon men who blaspheme God.

In the Bible, the prophet Isaiah spoke of this time and the reason for these great and awful judgments. These are the days you are, or will be living in shortly.

Isaiah 13:6-16 6 Wail, for the day of the Lord is at hand! It will come as destruction from the Almighty. 7 Therefore all hands will be limp, every man's heart will melt, 8 and they will be afraid. Pangs and sorrows will take hold of them; they will be in pain as a woman in childbirth; they will be amazed at one another; their faces will be like flames. 9 Behold, the day of the Lord comes, cruel, with both wrath and fierce anger, to lay the land desolate; and He will destroy its sinners from it. 10 For the stars of heaven and their constellations will not give their light; the sun will be darkened in its going forth, and the moon will not cause its light to shine. 11 "I will punish the world for its evil, and the wicked for their iniquity; I will halt the arrogance of the proud, and will lay low the haughtiness of the terrible. 12 I will make a mortal more rare than fine gold, a man more than the golden wedge of Ophir. 13 Therefore I will shake the heavens, and the earth will move out of her place, in the wrath of the Lord of hosts and in the day of

> *His fierce anger. 14 It shall be as the hunted gazelle, and as a sheep that no man takes up; every man will turn to his own people, and everyone will flee to his own land. 15 Everyone who is found will be thrust through, and everyone who is captured will fall by the sword. 16 Their children also will be dashed to pieces before their eyes; their houses will be plundered and their wives ravished.*

Are these horrific events unimaginable or unbelievable? Are they any more unbelievable than millions of people vanishing from the earth in a moment? These events will happen just as the Bible declares. Depending on what time in history you are reading this, these judgments may have already begun. But when do these judgments begin? What triggers the start of the judgments and the beginning of the Tribulation? The Bible holds the answers to these questions. If you want to know, keep reading.

Part Four—Section 3

In the first seal judgment, you read that a ruler known as the Antichrist sets out to conquer the world, and the world he indeed conquers—for a time. This man, also known in the Bible as the man of sin, the son of perdition, the lawless one, and the beast, will arise as a politician, a man of peace with the answers to the world's toughest issues. He emerges shortly after the Rapture.

The Bible declares that this man is a deceiver guided by Satan himself—likely indwelt by Satan at times. He will be a tool of the devil as the devil makes one last stand against God, attempting to become like God on the earth and make a mockery of Jesus Christ. Just as the prophet Isaiah spoke about God's judgment during the Tribulation, the prophet Daniel was also given insight by God about the time of the Tribulation, the rise of the Antichrist, and the evil schemes and purposes the Antichrist will accomplish during this time.

According to the Bible in the book of Daniel and Revelation, the Antichrist will come from a European nation, or a nation within what would be considered the revived Roman Empire *(Daniel 9:26)*. As the Tribulation progresses, the Antichrist begins to display great supernatural abilities through the power of Satan, as well as through trickery and deception. Then the day comes when he declares himself to be God and demands to be worshipped by the world *(Revelation 13)*. At that point, he will have the power and authority on the earth to make such demands as he has now united the world into a one world economy, religion, and government that he has absolute control over.

As the Antichrist gains power and influence, he stuns the world by single handedly solving the Middle East peace conflict in a day as he establishes a peace treaty for seven years with the nation Israel and her neighbors. According to Daniel, this seven year peace pact is what begins the start of the Tribulation *(Daniel 9:27)*. You can be assured that the man who brokers this deal is the Antichrist. When day one begins of this false peace, you have just lived through the first day of the Tribulation. Mark your calendar, because the ride and reign of terror is just beginning—only about 2554 more days to go. You do have an advantage though. You have the Bible, which spells out the chain of events that will take place and has the answers for receiving God's eternal mercy and grace, so that either through death or life you can one day enter His glorious kingdom as His child and not have to confront Him as His enemy.

To assist the Antichrist, Satan will inspire a helper which the Bible refers to as the "false prophet." The false prophet is a religious leader, possibly a priest, rabbi, or pastor of some kind. Some believe the Bible suggests that he may actually be a Jew. Satan gives the false prophet miraculous signs and wonders that he performs in front of the world. The false prophet's job will be to trick the world into believing that the Antichrist is their savior, ultimately that the Antichrist is God himself. The book of Revelation reveals the role of this false religious leader as he, the Antichrist, and Satan together form a union or mock trinity to deceive and conquer the world *(Revelation 13:1-18 and 19:20)*.

With this unholy force of power unleashed on the world, the Antichrist uses the world's technologies and advancements for his advantage to accomplish his evil purposes. He will use mass communication technologies such as TV, satellites, internet, and other social media to spread his cause and lies. He is able to unite a one world banking system and economy with a one world cashless currency over which he has ultimate control.

The book of Revelation states that if anyone is to buy, sell, be employed, or be able to function in this global economy they will be required to receive a mark (likely a tattoo or branding of some kind) on their forehead or right hand with the number, "666." This number is referred to in the Bible as the *"mark of the beast."* Having this mark will show total allegiance to the Antichrist and his government *(Revelation 13:16-18)*. Whatever you do, do not receive this mark. The Bible declares that whoever receives this mark cannot inherit God's kingdom when He returns. This mark shows that you are an enemy of Christ—a follower of the Antichrist. You will have chosen the wrong side if you decide to take this upon yourself.

It may seem crazy to not take the mark, since not taking it will drive you to poverty in an instant. But what is more valuable, your material assets or your eternal soul? Jesus once said, *"For what will it profit a man if he gains the whole world, and loses his own soul? Or what will a man give in exchange for his soul?" (Mark 8:36-37)* Would you pluck out your eyes or cut off your hands for the riches of the world? Of course you wouldn't. How much more valuable is your soul, or eternal essence and being that will never perish, compared to what you possess on the earth? Jesus also said, *"And do not fear those who kill the body but cannot kill the soul. But rather fear Him who is able to destroy both soul and body in hell." (Matthew 10:28)* These are questions you will quickly need to come to terms with regarding what your real priorities are.

This horrible time you are living in is just a mere season in eternity. It will pass shortly. Be brave, take courage, trust God and do what is right according to God's Word and not the ways of man or Satan. You will suffer, but your reward will be great if you choose to follow Christ in these last days. Jesus said, *"And behold, I am coming quickly, and My reward is with Me, to give to every one according to his work (Revelation 22:12).*

Part Four—Section 4

As horrible as evil, sin, and the power of Satan will be during this time, God's power will also be on glorious display in remarkable ways. The ultimate battle of good versus evil will be for all to see. Jesus once told His disciples that during the last days the gospel would be preached in all the world, and then the end would come *(Matthew 24:14)*. During the time of the Tribulation, God will go to great lengths to reach mankind with the truth of His Word and the message of eternal life.

The Bible makes mention of 144,000 saints of God, ordained by God to go out to preach the gospel of Christ throughout the world. These individuals will be Jews who have come to an understanding and saving grace in Jesus during this time. According to the Bible, there will be 12,000 representatives from the ancient twelve tribes of Israel who have the seal of God upon their lives as they go out to evangelize the world *(Revelation 7:1-8)*. Supernatural protection from God will be upon them. The Antichrist and his forces will not be able to harm these mighty chosen servants of the Most High.

 If you claim to follow Christ during these days, evidence of your faith in God will be revealed or tested depending on how you treat these chosen disciples of Christ, or any follower of Christ for that matter. Jesus once said of this time, that if you provide food, shelter, clothing, and care for the needs of these ones—Christ's brothers, it is just as if you are providing these amenities to Christ himself. If you deny them of these necessities, it is as if you are denying Christ and turning Him away. To reject these chosen servants of Christ during the Tribulation is the same as rejecting Christ, and that has eternally damning consequences *(Matthew 25:31-46)*. This will be a true test of your faith for Christ, because you will literally be putting your life on the line for assisting followers of Christ—enemies of the Antichrist. Make the right choice—follow Christ!

In chapter eleven of Revelation you can learn about two supernaturally gifted individuals sent to the earth by God to preach Christ and prophesy. They are known in Scripture as the "two witnesses." These men likely come from heaven and are believed by many who have studied Scripture to be Moses and Elijah, Moses and Enoch, or possibly two new prophets brought up in the last days. Regardless of who they are, they have a special mission by God. They are granted supernatural powers that they will execute as they preach the Word of God and prophesy to the world.

The two witnesses arrive on the scene shortly after the Tribulation begins and they prophesy exactly one thousand two hundred and sixty days. As they preach, if anyone attempts to harm them fire will come from their mouths and they kill anyone who comes against them. These two have the power to stop rain from falling, turn water into blood, and to strike the earth with all plagues as often as they desire.

At the end of their ministry, God allows them to be killed and their dead bodies will lie in the streets of Jerusalem. The world will celebrate and have parties for joy that these two prophets are lying dead in the street after tormenting the earth for the last three and a half years. Their bodies lie dead, untouched for three and a half days. Life then again enters their bodies and they stand to their feet as God resurrects them. Those who see this are overcome with fear as a voice from heaven cries out, *"Come up here."* The two witnesses will ascend into the sky on a cloud and go to heaven as their enemies watch in awe and fear. At that time, a great earthquake strikes the city of Jerusalem. A tenth of the city crumbles resulting in seven thousand deaths.

If the two witnesses don't grab your attention, you may be alarmed to see three angels that descend to the earth to preach the gospel and prophesy *(Revelation 14:6-13)*. Take heed to listen to the message of the angels. The first angel declares to every nation of the world with a loud voice, *"Fear God and give glory to Him, for the hour of His judgment has come; and worship Him who made heaven and earth, the sea and springs of water."*

Another angel will give warning for those who have, or may be thinking of following the Antichrist as he says:

> *"If anyone worships the beast and his image, and receives his mark on his forehead or on his hand, he himself shall also drink of the wine of the wrath of God, which is poured out full strength into the cup of His indignation. He shall be tormented with fire and brimstone in the presence of the holy angels and in the presence of the Lamb. And the smoke of their torment ascends forever and ever; and they have no rest day or night, who worship the beast and his image, and whoever receives the mark of his name."*

Is it possible there could be an atheist on the planet during this time? If you know one, you know a fool. *Psalm 53:1-4* declares:

> *The fool has said in his heart, "There is no God." They are corrupt, and have done abominable iniquity; There is none who does good. God looks down from heaven upon the children of men, to see if there are any who understand, who seek God. Every one of them has turned aside; They have together become corrupt; There is none who does good, No, not one.*

Be a wise child of God, seek Him and understand.

Part Four—Section 5

During the upcoming days and time of the Tribulation, you will see the world plagued with extremely horrific and terrible war. It is quite possible that many of the judgments and mass deaths spelled out in Revelation are a result of war, especially nuclear war.

There are several wars prophesied in Scripture that as of this writing have yet to occur. It is highly likely these future wars and battles facilitate the world scenario for the Antichrist to step in and make peace with Israel that starts the Tribulation. It is after all, Israel that these future prophetic battles encompass. Though Scripture does not state specifically when these wars will occur, there is evidence in Scripture to suggest these wars occur after the Rapture and before the Tribulation.

Isaiah chapter 17 declares the utter destruction and annihilation of the city of Damascus, Syria. Damascus is considered the oldest continuously inhabited city of the world at over 4000 years old. Damascus has seen war and has been ravaged and conquered over the centuries, but at no point has it ever ceased being a city in absolute ruin as indicated in *Isaiah 17:1 and 14*.

> *1 The burden against Damascus. "Behold, Damascus will cease from being a city, and it will be a ruinous heap. 14 Then behold, at eventide, trouble! And before the morning, he* (Damascus) *is no more. This is the portion of those who plunder us,* (Israel) *and those who rob us.*

This battle will be sudden, brief, and devastating. There is only one weapon in modern warfare capable of accomplishing the destruction described—a nuclear weapon. Syria will come against Israel and Israel will respond with overwhelming force. Damascus will be destroyed. Isaiah 17 also declares that Israel suffers extreme loss during this battle as they too lose cities in northern Israel (vs. 4-6). The loss that Israel experiences during this battle will get their attention and cause a stir to look to God for help (vs. 7-8).

Jeremiah 49:23-27 also speaks of this coming judgment against the city of Damascus as it states:

23 Against Damascus. "Hamath and Arpad are shamed, for they have heard bad news. They are fainthearted; there is trouble on the sea; it cannot be quiet. 24 Damascus has grown feeble; she turns to flee, and fear has seized her. Anguish and sorrows have taken her like a woman in labor. 25 Why is the city of praise not deserted, the city of My joy? 26 Therefore her young men shall fall in her streets, and all the men of war shall be cut off in that day," says the Lord of hosts. 27 "I will kindle a fire in the wall of Damascus, and it shall consume the palaces of Ben-Hadad."

There are two other future wars prophesied in Scripture found in *Psalm 83* and *Ezekiel 38 and 39*. Again, the timing of these wars and in what order they fall will be unknown until they are about to happen, but the Bible does reveal they will be in the last days. The Isaiah 17 battle could be part of the Psalm 83 war, it could come before it and lead to it, or it could stand alone. Many who have studied these wars and have been following events in the Middle East are suggesting as events unfold, that Psalm 83 follows Isaiah 17, followed by Ezekiel 38 also known as the Gog–Magog war.

Quite possibly, after Israel is humbled from the Isaiah 17 conflict, the events of Psalm 83 begin to unfold. Her Muslim neighbors will be furious that Israel has destroyed Damascus and in response, begin to plot the plunder of Israel.

Psalm 83:2-5 2 For behold, Your enemies make a tumult; and those who hate You have lifted up their head. 3 They have taken crafty counsel against Your people, and consulted together against Your sheltered ones. 4 They have said, "Come, and let us cut them off from being a nation, that the name of Israel may be remembered no more." 5 For they have consulted together with one consent; they form a confederacy against You:

The following verses (6-8) spell out the ancient border enemies of Israel that make this plot. Geographically, these ancient enemies are currently the West Bank, Jordan, Lebanon, Gaza, and Syria; mostly all of Israel's closest enemies. Their goal is plunder as spelled out in verse twelve: *Who said, "Let us take for ourselves the pastures of God for a possession."* Psalm 83 does not declare who wins this conflict, but be assured Israel will not lose any of these future battles. This has been promised by God in other scriptures elsewhere in the Bible such as *Zechariah 12:6-9* and *Amos 9:15*.

Psalm 83 could be a war, or it could be a precursor and initial plot for the Gog–Magog war of Ezekiel 38-39. This will be an expanded force of enemies against Israel to include none other than Russia, Iran, Turkey, Libya, Sudan, Kazakhstan, Uzbekistan, Kyrgyzstan, Turkmenistan, Tajikistan, and possibly Afghanistan, Azerbaijan, Armenia, Algeria, Tunisia, and Ethiopia. This is according to the ancient list of enemies from Ezekiel 38 that include Rosh, Persia, Magog, Meshech, Tubal, Gomer, Bethtogarmah, Put, and Cush.

The Gog–Magog war will be a glorious defeat of Israel's staunchest enemies, and show to the world the power of Israel's God. God alone miraculously destroys all who dare come against Israel—God's chosen nation from times past.

Here is a rundown of the Gog–Magog war as seen through the eyes of prophetic Scripture dictated by God to man (Ezekiel) nearly 2600 years ago.

Ezekiel 38: 10 "Thus says the Lord God; "On that day it shall come to pass that thoughts will arise in your mind, and you will make an evil plan: 16 You will come up against My people Israel like a cloud, to cover the land. It will be in the latter days that I will bring you against My land, so that the nations may know Me, when I am hallowed in you, O Gog, before their eyes." 18 "And it will come to pass at the same time, when Gog comes against the land of Israel," says the Lord God, "that My fury will show in My face. 21 I will call for a sword against Gog throughout all My mountains," says the Lord God. "Every man's sword will be against his brother. 22 And I will bring him to judgment with pestilence and bloodshed; I will rain down on him, on his troops, and on the many peoples who are with him, flooding rain, great hailstones, fire, and brimstone. 23 Thus I will magnify Myself and sanctify Myself, and I will be known in the eyes of many nations. Then they shall know that I am the Lord.'"

Ezekiel 39: 3 Then I will knock the bow out of your left hand, and cause the arrows to fall out of your right hand. 4 You shall fall upon the mountains of Israel, you and all your troops and the peoples who are with you; I will give you to birds of prey of every sort and to the beasts of the field to be devoured. 6 "And I will send fire on Magog and on those who live in security in the coastlands. Then they shall know that I am the Lord. 7 So I will make My holy name known in the midst of My people Israel, and I will not let them profane My holy name anymore. Then the nations shall know that I am the Lord, the Holy One in Israel.

What a tragic fate to those who think they can wipe Israel off the map and plunder their land. This is God's land given to His chosen people as an everlasting covenant. No one can take it away from them.

As you continue to read *Ezekiel 39*, what happens next is a strong indication as to when this war will take place. After the destruction of Israel's enemies, their weapons are scattered across the land and for seven years Israel will burn those weapons with *"many fires."* In reality, this is likely a huge governmental recycling project. Imagine the weapons of today's warfare—jets, tanks, missiles, chemicals, fuels, and other toxic debris scattered in your back yard, school yard, and parks. The debris will be overwhelming, and what a huge mess it will be.

Also, dead bodies will be found lying everywhere. *Ezekiel 39:11-16* describes the burial process needed to process such a large amount of bodies. It takes seven months to cleanse the land and bury the bodies. According to Scripture, the job requires search parties scouring the land, picking up bodies, pieces of bodies and bones, carefully marking them and then gathering them for burial.

The fact that Scripture indicates that it takes seven years to clean up the weapons is a clue revealing this war has to be at least three and a half years before the Tribulation begins. Remember, the last three and a half years of the Tribulation—The Great Tribulation, is the time when the Antichrist hunts down Jews and kills two-thirds of them *(Zechariah 13:8-9)*. The Jews are on the run and are fleeing Jerusalem in droves. Up to then, they were at peace with the world under the protection of the Antichrist. The Antichrist then breaks the seven year peace treaty he made with them, desecrates their holy temple, and declares himself to be God. There is no way that the nation would still be organized and intact to conduct the burning or recycling of the fallen weapons during the last half of the Tribulation after the Antichrist has declared all-out war on them. Also, if this war were to occur after the start of the Tribulation, then the seven years needed to burn the weapons would extend into the millenial kingdom—a very unlikely scenario.

The timing of the Gog-Magog war fits nicely at least three and a half years before the Tribulation. This gives the Antichrist the opportunity to establish the peace treaty with Israel prophesied by Daniel. The world will no doubt be polarized and in fear from the supernatural defeat God displayed against Israel's enemies. With the Russian and Muslim militaries having been utterly destroyed, the Antichrist will step right in to fill that role as world leader and peace maker. Hello Tribulation!

Part Four—Section 6

Probably the most noted future war or battle that many have heard about to some degree is the battle of Armageddon. In recent years, the title "Armageddon" has gotten the attention of Hollywood and apocalyptic writers who refer to Armageddon as some earth destroying catastrophic event such as an asteroid striking the earth, worldwide nuclear war, or some other idea founded on nothing but imagination. In fact, many who have studied the Bible all their life assume Armageddon to be a future war to end all wars. Describing Armageddon as a "war" may be an inaccurate term for the nature of the event. The truth about Armageddon is that it will not end up being a war at all, but rather a righteous massacre of evil.

The phrase "battle of Armageddon," or "war of Armageddon" is not even mentioned in the Bible. The term Armageddon is an English translation for the Hebrew word Har-Magedon found in *Revelation 16:16*. The word literally means Mount of Megiddo. There was once an ancient fortress on this Mount called Megiddo that controlled the valley of Jezreel, a huge valley running diagonally across Israel from the Jordan River to Haifa. This valley is now known as the valley of Megiddo, or valley of Armageddon and is an absolute perfect location for an all-out military battle.

During the last days of the Tribulation, the Antichrist and militaries of the world gather in the great valley of Megiddo in preparation for a large scale war. If you remember the sixth bowl judgment, the Euphrates River dries up which allows a two hundred million man army from the east to march across the river for entrance into Israel and the place prepared for battle (*Revelation 16:12-16*). Just as the buttons and triggers are about to be pushed to launch this massive offensive against Christ, the Lord Jesus returns riding a white horse with the armies of heaven. He steps foot on the Mount of Olives near Jerusalem and the mountain literally splits in two (*Zechariah 14:4*). The largest earthquake ever then takes place, which levels mountains and islands all over the world—the seventh bowl judgment. It is also at this time that Jesus Christ lays waist the armies assembled for battle in the valley. This great battle will be over before it ever begins. The Lord completely annihilates and obliterates all who assemble against Him at Armageddon in a victorious slaughter of evil.

Zechariah 14:12 describes their destruction.

And it shall be the plague with which the Lord will strike all the people who fought against Jerusalem: their flesh shall dissolve while they stand on their feet, their eyes shall dissolve in their sockets, and their tongues shall dissolve in their mouths. When the Lord returns He will *"consume with the breath of His mouth and destroy with the brightness of His coming" (2 Thessalonians 2:8).*

Christ's entrance as He descends to the earth is unmistakable and to say "powerful" would be an understatement.

Revelation 19:11-16 11 Now I saw heaven opened, and behold, a white horse. And He who sat on him was called Faithful and True, and in righteousness He judges and makes war. 12 His eyes were like a flame of fire, and on His head were many crowns. He had a name written that no one knew except Himself. 13 He was clothed with a robe dipped in blood, and His name is called the Word of God. 14 And the armies in heaven, clothed in fine linen, white and clean, followed Him on white horses. 15 Now out of His mouth goes a sharp sword, that with it He should strike the nations. And He Himself will rule them with a rod of iron. He Himself treads the winepress of the fierceness and wrath of Almighty God. 16 And He has on His robe and on His thigh a name written: KING OF KINGS AND LORD OF LORDS.

As for the Antichrist, the false prophet, and Satan—their doomed fate is sealed.

Revelation 19:19-20 19 And I saw the beast, (the Antichrist) *the kings of the earth, and their armies, gathered together to make war against Him who sat on the horse and against His army. 20 Then the beast was captured, and with him the false prophet who worked signs in his presence, by which he deceived those who received the mark of the beast and those who worshipped his image. These two were cast alive into the lake of fire burning with brimstone.*

Revelation 20:1-3 1 Then I saw an angel coming down from heaven, having the key to the bottomless pit and a great chain in his hand. 2 He laid hold of the dragon, that serpent of old, who is the Devil and Satan, and bound him for a thousand years; 3 and he cast him into the bottomless pit, and shut him up, and set a seal on him, so that he should deceive the nations no more till the thousand years were finished. But after these things he must be released for a little while.

Part Four—Section 7

The great mystery of "Armageddon" can be summed up as the "triumphant return of the Lord." Armageddon is not the destruction of the world, but rather the saving of the world by Jesus Christ as He puts an end to the time of the Tribulation, Satan, and all those who seek to do evil. If you are left standing when the smoke of God's wrath clears at His return, you are one of three kinds of people:

1. A remnant of the Jewish people who have come to terms with Christ as their Messiah and have repented for their rejection of Him.

2. A gentile, or non-Jewish follower of Jesus Christ who managed to survive the persecution and genocide of the Antichrist

3. A surviving follower of the Antichrist who has taken his mark and has rejected Christ. Jews, who still have not accepted Christ, fall into this category as well.

If you are one of the first two groups, you are welcomed into Christ's new kingdom and will be an active participant in the plans He has for restoring humanity and civilization. If you are in the latter group, someone who has not repented of sin and received Christ's forgiveness through faith in Him, then you will be a part of what Christ does next on the earth.

Scripture clearly says what happens to those who have rejected Christ at His coming. Jesus refers to the surviving remnant as sheep and goats. Christ is the Good Shepherd, so the sheep are His children whom He leads into everlasting life. Goats are surely different from sheep in that sheep are generally calm and gentle creatures, whereas goats can be rowdy and rambunctious, making them difficult to herd with sheep. Because goats can easily upset the sheep as they graze or rest together, the shepherd needs to separate them if he at all cares for his sheep as a good shepherd should. Jesus Christ will set apart the sheep from the goats. He leads the sheep with His right hand into everlasting pastures, and casts the goats—the unbelieving remnant of humanity, into eternal torment and punishment. The two cannot dwell together in His perfect kingdom of peace and justice.

Jesus in His own words was very direct about this truth.

Matthew 24:31 And He will send His angels with a great sound of a trumpet, and they will gather together His elect from the four winds, from one end of heaven to the other.

Matthew 25:31-34 31 "When the Son of Man comes in His glory, and all the holy angels with Him, then He will sit on the throne of His glory. 32 All the nations will be gathered before Him, and He will separate them one from another, as a shepherd divides his sheep from the goats. 33 And He will set the sheep on His right hand, but the goats on the left. 34 Then the King will say to those on His right hand, 'Come, you blessed of My Father, inherit the kingdom prepared for you from the foundation of the world:

Matthew 13:41-43, 47-50 41 The Son of Man will send out His angels, and they will gather out of His kingdom all things that offend, and those who practice lawlessness, 42 and will cast them into the furnace of fire. There will be wailing and gnashing of teeth. 43 Then the righteous will shine forth as the sun in the kingdom of their Father. He who has ears to hear, let him hear! 47 "Again, the kingdom of heaven is like a dragnet that was cast into the sea and gathered some of every kind, 48 which, when it was full, they drew to shore; and they sat down and gathered the good into vessels, but threw the bad away. 49 So it will be at the end of the age. The angels will come forth, separate the wicked from among the just, 50 and cast them into the furnace of fire. There will be wailing and gnashing of teeth."

Part Four—Section 8

The kingdom of Jesus Christ has now come to planet earth. He is here as the world's Supreme Ruler and King. Things will be done His way, according to His time, and for His purposes. What this kingdom fully looks like we will not know until it unfolds, though the Bible gives us many insights into Christ's reign on the earth.

A question one might ask is, "How is the world going to convert from the carnage and destruction it has seen, to a place of peace, prosperity, and justice in such as short amount of time?" The damage to infrastructure world-wide, not to mention the filth and mess from war and disasters will be overwhelming. What we can learn from the Bible in the book of Daniel is that there is a transition period of seventy-five days from the time Christ returns, until the official start of His millennial reign. This will be a time for God to "clean house."

At exactly the mid-point of the Tribulation the Antichrist desecrates the Jews Holy temple and declares himself to be God, erecting a statue of himself which he demands to be worshipped. From that exact day there is 1260 days left in the Tribulation—the last three and a half years.

Daniel 12:11-12 states:

> 11 *"And from the time that the daily sacrifice is taken away, and the abomination of desolation is set up,* (Antichrist's statue) *there shall be one thousand two hundred and ninety days. 12 Blessed is he who waits, and comes to the one thousand three hundred and thirty-five days.*

1335 days minus the 1260 days left of the Tribulation leaves a time period of seventy-five days. Christ returns at about the 1260 day mark and the statue of abomination is taken down at 1290 days, thirty days after the return. There is yet then forty-five more days until the 1335 day mark when the Millennium officially begins. If that sounds confusing, it is. Read it again.

So what will be going on during this seventy-five day transition period? There is much that needs to be accomplished at the onset of Christ's return. Here is what will likely be taking place during that time.

- The Antichrist, false prophet, Satan, and his demonic hordes are captured, bound, and secured in the place God has prepared for them *(Revelation 19:19-20, 20:1-3)*.

- Christ judges the surviving Jewish people. He accepts those who have repented and believed while casting away the rebellious, unaccepting stragglers likely in the fashion He deals with the unbelieving gentiles *(Ezekiel 20:33-38)*.

- Christ judges the gentile nations separating the believers from the unbelievers—the sheep and goat judgment *(Matthew 25:31-34)*.

- Resurrection: Old Testament saints such as Daniel and Joseph, as well as Tribulation saints—Christ followers who died during the Tribulation, receive their eternal, glorified, resurrected physical bodies just as the Church of Christ received at the Rapture *(Daniel 12:2,13 and Revelation 20:4)*.

- Christ's earthly government is structured. Christ's saints who have been resurrected and glorified will have an integral part in reigning and ruling with Christ on the earth. His saints are likely going to be governors, rulers, judges, and overseers placed throughout the earth. Their placement and position may be established during this time *(Revelation 20:4-6 and 5:10)*.

- Cleansing the land: The filth, decay, and destruction left behind from the world's judgment will in some means be purged from the earth. It is quite possible that the seventh bowl judgment (the great earthquake) assists in this as islands and mountains will crumble and disappear *(Revelation 16:18-20)*. The quake is so great that earth's topography will be changed. The earth literally swallows up vast cities and nations. The clean-up could also be supernatural; accomplished by Christ, angels, and glorified saints.

Part Four—Section 9

Christ's rule as King of the earth is often referred to as His "millennial reign," or time of the Millennium. The Bible declares that this period of Christ physically ruling the earth in this fashion literally lasts one thousand years, or one millennium. During this time, Satan and the demons are locked in hell and are restricted from interfering or obstructing the work of Christ in any way. The only people left on the planet when the Millennium begins are followers of Jesus who love, serve, and welcome His Lordship.

Life will be much different than humanity has ever known it. Even in the Garden of Eden, as good as that was, Adam and Eve were still plagued with the father of lies—Satan. Though it will be wonderful compared to what humanity has known; it won't be perfect. Humanity will still be cursed with their inherent desire to sin, the nature they were born with that has been passed down to us since the fall of Adam. They won't have the tempter, but they will have the sinful passions of the flesh. Those desires should be much easier to curb without the temptations of Satan and being exposed to rampant sin as we are today.

Much of the curse of Adam that we have long struggled with in this life is partially lifted during the Millennium. For example, longevity of life will be prolonged. Man will live increased years such as it was in the days of Noah and prior. Sickness, disease, and infirmities for the most part will be eradicated and nature will appear to blossom in "*Garden of Eden*" like fashion *(Ezekiel 36:35)*. Even wild animals that would normally devour one another will graze together in harmony. Peace will be prevalent over the face of the earth, and war a thing of the past. Starvation, slavery, abortion, sexual immorality, crime, suicide, hatred, drug abuse, and all the common evils and treachery of today's world will not be tolerated. If those evils do begin to show their head, they will be crushed by Christ's authority.

Christ's rule will encompass the globe and His glory and majesty will be inescapable *(Isaiah 11:9)*. Again, sin and death will still be a part of humanity. Sin will have consequences as it always has, but those consequences will be quite severe. The Bible indicates that Christ will rule the nations with a *"rod of iron" (Revelation 2:27, 12:5, 19:15 and Psalm 2:9)*. What that exactly looks like we will someday find out. It would be safe to say that life on earth will be as close to paradise as it can get, while man still possesses a sinful human nature.

Here are a few among many intriguing verses about the time of the Millennium. If you are currently living through the Tribulation, let these scriptures provide you with comfort and assurance for the hope of better days ahead.

> *Isaiah 9:6-7 6 For unto us a Child is born, unto us a Son is given; and the government will be upon His shoulder. And His name will be called Wonderful Counselor, Mighty God, Everlasting Father, Prince of Peace. 7 Of the increase of His government and peace there will be no end, upon the throne of David and over His kingdom, to order it and establish it with judgment and justice from that time forward, even forever. The zeal of the Lord of hosts will perform this.*

> *Daniel 7:13-14 13 "I was watching in the night visions, and behold, One like the Son of Man, coming with the clouds of heaven! He came to the Ancient of Days, and they brought Him near before Him. 14 Then to Him was given dominion and glory and a kingdom, that all peoples, nations, and languages should serve Him. His dominion is an everlasting dominion, which shall not pass away, and His kingdom the one which shall not be destroyed.*

> *Micah 4:3-4 3 He shall judge between many peoples, and rebuke strong nations afar off; they shall beat their swords into plowshares, and their spears into pruning hooks; nation shall not lift up sword against nation, neither shall they learn war anymore. 4 But everyone shall sit under his vine and under his fig tree, and no one shall make them afraid; for the mouth of the Lord of hosts has spoken.*

Isaiah 35:1,6,7 1 The wilderness and the wasteland shall be glad for them, and the desert shall rejoice and blossom as the rose; 6 …For waters shall burst forth in the wilderness, and streams in the desert. 7 The parched ground shall become a pool, and the thirsty land springs of water…

Isaiah 65:20-22 20 "No more shall an infant from there live but a few days, nor an old man who has not fulfilled his days; for the child shall die one hundred years old, but the sinner being one hundred years old shall be accursed. 21 They shall build houses and inhabit them; they shall plant vineyards and eat their fruit. 22 They shall not build and another inhabit; they shall not plant and another eat; for as the days of a tree, so shall be the days of My people, and My elect shall long enjoy the work of their hands.

Isaiah 29:18, 33:24, 35:5-6 29:18 In that day the deaf shall hear the words of the book, and the eyes of the blind shall see out of obscurity and out of darkness. 33:24 And the inhabitant will not say, "I am sick"; the people who dwell in it will be forgiven their iniquity. 35:5 Then the eyes of the blind shall be opened, and the ears of the deaf shall be unstopped. 6 Then the lame shall leap like a deer, and the tongue of the dumb sing…

Isaiah 11:6-8 6 "The wolf also shall dwell with the lamb, the leopard shall lie down with the young goat, the calf and the young lion and the fatling together; and a little child shall lead them. 7 The cow and the bear shall graze; their young ones shall lie down together; and the lion shall eat straw like the ox. 8 The nursing child shall play by the cobra's hole, and the weaned child shall put his hand in the viper's den.

Jeremiah 31:12-14 12 …Their souls shall be like a well-watered garden, and they shall sorrow no more at all. 13 "Then shall the virgin rejoice in the dance, and the young men and the old, together; for I will turn their mourning to joy, will comfort them, and make them rejoice rather than sorrow. 14 I will satiate the soul of the priests with abundance, and My people shall be satisfied with My goodness, says the Lord."

What will your part be in Christ's millennial kingdom? If you have missed the Rapture and are a new believer in Christ and are, or are about to be going through the time of the Tribulation, have courage and take heart. Jesus Christ has your back. Whether you live or die during the Tribulation, the Lord has a magnificent plan spelled out in the Bible for your future.

Do not fear death during the Tribulation. It will be a wonderful gift from the Lord, because immediately upon death you will be ushered into God's throne room where you will see your Creator face to face. When Christ returns, you will return with Him and your physical dead body will be resurrected. You will receive a new, glorified, physical body that will never taste death again. This body will have unbelievable supernatural abilities not bound to the laws of gravity or nature. It will be a body just like Jesus Christ's *(1 John 3:2)*! No more will you ever suffer pain, exhaustion, sickness, or grief. Your role in Christ's millennial reign on the earth is clearly spelled out in Scripture. You will be used mightily as a treasured saint of the Most High as revealed in *Revelation 20:4-6.*

> *4 ... Then I saw the souls of those who had been beheaded for their witness to Jesus and for the word of God, who had not worshipped the beast or his image, and had not received his mark on their foreheads or on their hands. And they lived and reigned with Christ for a thousand years. 6 ...they shall be priests of God and of Christ, and shall reign with Him a thousand years.*

If the Lord allows you to survive the Tribulation, your role in the Millennium will be different. You will be rare, special, and valued like a precious gem. With your fleshly, natural eyes you will see Jesus Christ in person, a privilege no one has had for nearly two thousand years. You will be the first to see Him take on His role as King of Kings and Lord of Lords as He establishes His kingdom upon the earth. If you have any injuries, diseases, or maladies, you will receive supernatural healing from Christ, or one of His emissaries either angelic or glorified. Your physical life will be changed and it will be extended and enhanced greatly. It is likely if you are aged that you will notice strength, energy, and vitality return to your body. Wrinkles will fade, hair may receive color, as well as sight and hearing will return to what you had in your younger years. You will be allowed to live out your days in peace and prosperity and will have an active part in renewing humanity under Christ's Lordship.

What an honor it will be for you to serve Christ as King and receive the blessings that are promised to all who follow Him as He restores the earth and humanity to conditions that He finds favorable. The terrible days you have previously experienced will begin to fade as you find a confidence and assurance under the Lordship of Christ that you never knew possible. What a blessing it will be to participate in this magnificent kingdom. The Creator of the universe will be your King and Lord. Just think about that.

Part Four—Section 10

As good as life will be during the Millennium, life again will be exposed to extreme evil at the completion of this time, but just briefly. Here is what Scripture says will happen at the very end of the Millennium.

> *Revelation 20:7-10 7 Now when the thousand years have expired, Satan will be released from his prison 8 and will go out to deceive the nations which are in the four corners of the earth, Gog and Magog, to gather them together to battle, whose number is as the sand of the sea. 9 They went up on the breadth of the earth and surrounded the camp of the saints and the beloved city. And fire came down from God out of heaven and devoured them. 10 The devil, who deceived them, was cast into the lake of fire and brimstone where the beast and false prophet are. And they will be tormented day and night forever and ever.*

As you and other followers of Christ enter the Millennium, you will be tasked with repopulating the planet. Over time, the population on earth will explode as death will now be curtailed and life will be expanded to hundreds of years. The children born during this time will be privileged to say the least, but unlike you, they won't fully grasp the concepts of the evil nature of sin, or the temptations of Satan as you experienced in your former days. Many will begin to take for granted the blessings of God. Their fleshly desires will bring out their fallen human nature and sinful passions. Though an outward expression of those passions will not be tolerated, an inward burning of doubt, power, greed, lust, and hate will be brewing.

When the tempter gets loosed, Satan will have a prime target ready to latch on to whatever deception and lie he will throw their way. Whatever it is, the deception is so great that an uncountable number of souls fall for the lie and an attempt will be made to overthrow Christ's government. How foolish this endeavor will be. Nonetheless, the consequences are deserved as the rebels are utterly annihilated and cast into the lake of fire along with Satan.

As good as man thinks he can get, and the greatness man thinks he can achieve in what would be considered a near perfect environment, this will expose the truth of man's total depravity and wicked heart. This truth cannot be escaped. The time of the Millennium is a perfect example of this. Christ will have given mankind every tool he supposedly needs to quench the desire to sin, live for righteousness, and pursue God. Even though God in the flesh is living with man on the earth, manifesting His greatness, kindness, and mercy to the fullest extent, man's own evil desires for the pursuit of perfection without God will be on full display for all creation to see at the end of the Millennium.

The Millennium in its entirety can be seen as an object lesson to show that man cannot save himself by his own pursuits. Man is inherently wicked and in desperate need of a Savior. Christ's sacrifice on the cross for the redemption and forgiveness of man's sin will be proven to be the only way man can be restored to a perfect relationship and unity with God. Christ is all that mankind needs. He created us and He desires to save His creation. We cannot save ourselves. Aside from Christ, we are absolutely destitute and have no purpose in creation; yet He loves each one of us as if we were the only person He ever created. In the beginning man was fully responsible for destroying his relationship with God through sin. In the end God is fully responsible for saving His relationship with man through Christ. It all points to the cross. Thank you Lord for the restoration and new creation you offer to each one of us, considering that we deserve none of it on our own merits.

> *Romans 5:6-11 6 For when we were still without strength, in due time Christ died for the ungodly. 7 For scarcely for a righteous man will one die; yet perhaps a good man someone would even dare to die. 8 But God demonstrates His own love toward us, in that while we were still sinners, Christ died for us. 9 Much more then, having now been justified by His blood, we shall be saved from wrath through Him. 10 For if when we were enemies we were reconciled to God through the death of His Son, much more, having been reconciled, we shall be saved by His life. 11 And not only that, but we also rejoice in God through our Lord Jesus Christ, through whom we have now received the reconciliation.*

Part Four—Section 11

At the conclusion of the Millennium a final resurrection of the dead occurs. Believers in Christ who have died during the Millennium are resurrected at this time just as all the redeemed who have been previously resurrected. These resurrections are referred to in Scripture as the *first resurrection (Revelation 20:6)*. The first resurrection is a picture of ancient Middle Eastern harvest time and occurs essentially in three phases—the first fruits, the general harvest, and the gleaning. Christ was the first fruits of the resurrection *(1 Corinthians 15:23)*. The resurrection of the Church at the Rapture is the general harvest resurrection. Tribulation and Old Testament saints are resurrected at the end of the Tribulation followed by the millennial saints. They are all part of the gleaning harvest and the very last to be resurrected to eternal glory as part of the first resurrection.

The second resurrection, also called the *second death*, then occurs and is one that no believer in Christ will be a part of. Unfortunately, this is the resurrection of the wicked dead. They are those who are not, and have never been a part of Christ. They have rejected His offer of salvation. Once their souls have been reunited with their physical resurrected bodies, now prepared for eternity, they are judged by the Lord Jesus based on the works they did while on the earth. This judgment in Scripture is called the *Great White Throne judgment*.

All those who enter this judgment will be found to fall short of God's perfect standards and are declared guilty. No good thing they have ever done can make up for the sin that tarnishes their soul. Christ's blood sacrifice that He offered them was not received. When Father God looks at the representation of their earthly life, He sees their sins as opposed to seeing Christ's sacrifice given to them in their stead. Based on their sin, they cannot inherit Christ's eternal kingdom and must be cast into the place prepared for Satan, the demons, and followers of Satan—the lake of fire.

For eternity they dwell in the lake of fire never being fully consumed by the fires. Their eternal resurrected bodies will never perish. Being forever separated from God and in torment, knowing there is no second chance and without hope, they will languish in the memories of missed opportunities where they had heard about and rejected Christ. They chose to embellish their sinful passions, as opposed to following the laws of God placed upon the hearts and conscience of everyone ever created *(Romans 2:14-16)*. Their rejection, or apathy towards that which was holy, true, and righteous seal their eternal doom *(Romans 1:18-21)*.

This judgment also constitutes the level of torment they will face for eternity, some more severe than others based on their wickedness. In this, as sad and awful as their fate is, Christ will ultimately receive glory, praise, and honor for this judgment. Everything Christ does is just, fair, and perfect. Christ is glorified in His judgments as much as He is in His gift of salvation and other holy attributes.

Revelation 20:11-15 11 Then I saw a great white throne and Him who sat on it, from whose face the earth and the heaven fled away. And there was found no place for them. 12 And I saw the dead, small and great, standing before God, and books were opened. And another book was opened, which is the Book of Life. And the dead were judged according to their works, by the things which were written in the books. 13 The sea gave up the dead who were in it, and Death and Hades delivered up the dead who were in them. And they were judged, each one according to his works. 14 Then Death and Hades were cast into the lake of fire. This is the second death. 15 And anyone not found written in the Book of Life was cast into the lake of fire.

Romans 1:18-21 18 For the wrath of God is revealed from heaven against all ungodliness and unrighteousness of men, who suppress the truth in unrighteousness, 19 because what may be known of God is manifest in them, for God has shown it to them. 20 For since the creation of the world His invisible attributes are clearly seen, being understood by the things that are made, even His eternal power and Godhead, so that they are without excuse, 21 because, although they knew God, they did not glorify Him as God, nor were thankful, but became futile in their thoughts, and their foolish hearts were darkened.

Part Four—Section 12

Now if you have been wondering how the story of the Bible ends, or are wondering why Christ only reigns on the earth for one thousand years, you will want to know what happens next. Absolute beauty and perfection is what happens next. The truth is, the story is just beginning. Time as we have known it is coming to an end and what is unfolding is the continuity of eternity. This thing that we have called "life on planet earth" has been but a wrinkle in the fabric of eternity.

All of this was created and done for one purpose and one purpose only—for God to reveal and demonstrate His glory and holy attributes to His creation, so that He Himself can be glorified. God as represented through the Heavenly Father, Christ the Son, and the Holy Spirit had pushed the pause button, so to speak, on what He had been doing in eternity past. After the Millennium, He will again put things back in play, but now a better, perfect, and clearer understanding of who He is and what He stands for is on record and display. All His creation now and forever will give Him glory, praise, and honor for what He has done and who He is.

After Christ has dealt with judging the sins of man and has vanquished all those who practice lawlessness, it is then time for Him to cure the curse that has for so long been placed upon the earth. The consequence of sin has not only sickened mankind, but has ransacked nature, the earth, and even the universe *(Romans 8:20-22)*. The Bible makes it clear that at the end of the age, God will do away with this sin-stained earth and universe and start over with a new creation—one that is incorruptible, perfect, and never again to be tainted with sin's disease.

Only Scripture can best explain and reveal this future cleansing of the universe.

> *Isaiah 65:17 and 66:22 and 51:6 65:17 "For behold, I create new heavens and a new earth; and the former shall not be remembered or come to mind. 66:22 "For as the new heavens and the*

new earth which I will make shall remain before Me," says the Lord, "so shall your descendants and your name remain. 51:6 Lift up your eyes to the heavens, and look on the earth beneath. For the heavens will vanish away like smoke, the earth will grow old like a garment...

2 Peter 3:7,10,13 7 But the heavens and the earth which are now preserved by the same word, are reserved for fire until the day of judgment and perdition of ungodly men. 10 But the day of the Lord will come as a thief in the night, in which the heavens will pass away with a great noise, and the elements will melt with fervent heat; both the earth and the works that are in it will be burned up. 13 Nevertheless we, according to His promise, look for new heavens and a new earth in which righteousness dwells.

Revelation 21:1-5 1 Now I saw a new heaven and a new earth, for the first heaven and the first earth had passed away. Also there was no more sea. 2 Then I, John, saw the holy city, New Jerusalem, coming down out of heaven from God, prepared as a bride adorned for her husband. 3 And I heard a loud voice from heaven saying, "Behold, the tabernacle of God is with men, and He will dwell with them, and they shall be His people. God Himself will be with them and be their God. 4 And God will wipe away every tear from their eyes; there shall be no more death, nor sorrow, nor crying. There shall be no more pain, for the former things have passed away." 5 Then He who sat on the throne said, "Behold, I make all things new." And He said to me, "Write, for these words are true and faithful."

Unlike previous judgments on the earth which were meant to punish, judge, and destroy, the creation of this new earth is not a judgment to destroy the old earth. When God originally created the earth and said it was "good," it was a perfect place of habitation for His new creation. It then became cursed with sin. This is again a creation of a perfect earth suitable for heavenly, eternal inhabitants, though the new earth will never be cursed with sin or anything evil. It is a renewal, a purification, and glorification of God's physical world. At the end of the Millennium when this happens, God will supernaturally remove all the humans from the planet and probably the animal kingdom as well, while He fashions this new earth and universe to perfection.

What becomes of the humans who were alive at the end of the Millennium? Do these humans receive glorified bodies, or will they retain their earthly bodies they were born with? Will they continue to propagate the human species for all eternity? Do their descendants populate other planets across the galaxies? These are all legitimate and profound questions that the Bible just does not give answers to, but are fascinating to think about.

The Bible declares that God's heavenly city—the New Jerusalem will come down and be placed on this new planet earth. Here, God will dwell on earth with all of His saints from all times, angels, and other heavenly creatures. Heaven will literally encompass the globe and the New Jerusalem will be the capital city.

Part Four—Section 13

Contemplating eternity and the plans God has is nearly unfathomable for our minds to comprehend in these fallen vessels. Scripture opens our mind to unimaginable realities yet to come. We are encouraged by this one verse in particular in *1 Corinthians 2:9* which says, *But as it is written: "Eye has not seen, nor ear heard, nor have entered into the heart of man the things which God has prepared for those who love Him."*

Though we don't yet know what all these *"things"* are that God has prepared for us, the book of Revelation does reveal some very marvelous and specific facts about the heavenly city.

> *Revelation 21:10-21 10 And he carried me away in the Spirit to a great and high mountain, and showed me the great city, the holy Jerusalem, descending out of heaven from God, 11 having the glory of God. Her light was like a most precious stone, like a jasper stone, clear as crystal. 12 Also she had a great and high wall with twelve gates, and twelve angels at the gates, and names written on them, which are the names of the twelve tribes of the children of Israel: 13 three gates on the east, three gates on the north, three gates on the south, and three gates on the west. 14 Now the wall of the city had twelve foundations, and on them were the names of the twelve apostles of the Lamb. 15 And he who talked with me had a gold reed to measure the city, its gates, and its wall. 16 The city is laid out as a square; its length is as great as its breadth. And he measured the city with the reed: twelve thousand furlongs. Its length, breadth, and height are equal. 17 Then he measured its wall: one hundred and forty-four cubits, according to the measure of a man, that is, of an angel. 18 The construction of its wall was of jasper; and the city was pure gold, like clear glass. 19 The foundations of the wall of the city were adorned with all kinds of precious stones: the first foundation was jasper, the second sapphire, the third chalcedony, the fourth emerald, 20 the fifth sardonyx, the sixth sardius, the seventh chrysolite, the eighth beryl, the ninth topaz, the tenth chrysoprase, the eleventh jacinth, and the twelfth*

amethyst. 21 The twelve gates were twelve pearls: each individual gate was of one pearl. And the street of the city was pure gold, like transparent glass.

Let's first consider the enormous size and shape of the New Jerusalem. As Scripture says, the city of heaven is laid out in the form of a cube. It is square and has the same dimensions in all directions. The length given is 12,000 furlongs, which equates to 1500 miles in every direction—1500 miles wide, long, and high. If the city were placed on top of the United States, it would stretch from Canada to the Gulf of Mexico and from New York to Colorado.

To grasp the magnitude of the city's height, consider this: The first layer of the earth's atmosphere, the troposphere, is where our weather occurs. It extends from the ground up to about eleven miles, or 58,000 feet. After several more layers, the atmosphere concludes in the exosphere stopping at about 800 miles above the surface of the earth. Beyond that, everything is just considered outer space. If the city of heaven were placed on our current earth, it would extend above the exosphere and reach up another 700 miles into outer space! If you were to try to climb the city you would run out of usable oxygen at about 26,000 feet—unable to breathe. From there, you would only have to climb another 7,894,000 feet to reach the top.

Another way to think of it is this. If the city of heaven were turned into a sphere with its circular edges touching on each of the eight corners of the cubical city, it would be equivalent in size to earth's moon. Needless to say, the future earth the Lord creates will likely be substantially larger than our current earth. The New Jerusalem would be grossly out of proportion in size to the earth we now inhabit.

The volume inside the city is vast. You might ask if there will be enough room for everyone. If just twenty-five percent of the city was devoted to housing twenty billion people, then each person would be allowed a space of about seventy cubic acres. Two hundred billion people could each occupy seven cubic acres. Would that be enough room for you?

Jesus once told His disciples, *In my Father's house are many mansions; if it were not so, I would have told you. And if I go and prepare* a place for you, I will come again and receive you to Myself; that where I am, there you may be also (John 14:2-3). What a glorious thought to be assured that the Creator of the universe is creating a place for us to live in His home—your home.

For just about everyone who has ever had the privilege of living in a safe and secure home, a place they could find comfort and rest, they would say that their home was the safest, most relaxing place they could possibly be; hence the saying, "There's no place like home." In examining this description of heaven in Revelation it is quite clear that this future home of ours, the New Jerusalem, will be beyond the idea of a safe and secure home.

According to *Revelation 21* the walls of the city are 216 feet thick, or 144 cubits. At each of the twelve gates of the city a mighty angel is posted as a guardian and ministering servant of God. The gates of the city will never be shut and there will never be anything to enter the city *that defiles, or causes an abomination, or a lie.* There is no night in the New Jerusalem and the glory of Jesus Christ is what gives the city its light.

Revelation 22:1-5 concludes the majestic description of this city and its eternally sustaining qualities.

> *1 And he showed me a pure river of water of life, clear as crystal, proceeding from the throne of God and of the Lamb. 2 In the middle of its street, and on either side of the river, was the tree of life, which bore twelve fruits, each tree yielding its fruit every month. The leaves of the tree were for the healing of the nations. 3 And there shall be no more curse, but the throne of God and of the Lamb shall be in it, and His servants shall serve Him. 4 They shall see His face, and His name shall be on their foreheads. 5 There shall be no night there: they need no lamp nor light of the sun, for the Lord God gives them light. And they shall reign forever and ever.*

Absolute beauty, splendor, majesty, and perfection are a few words to describe just a glimpse from Scripture about what awaits us in our heavenly home. From streets of gold, walls of jasper, gates of pearls, to a crystal clear and pure river of life and the famous tree of life, these pictures of heaven almost seem surreal, or sound too good to be true. However, it is one of the most significant truths we will ever come to know. As wonderful as all the aesthetics of heaven that we will experience with our senses; the most magnificent wonder is that we will live with God forever in this place.

Being able to learn about God and experience Him to the fullest extent is an activity that will be the most rewarding and thrilling for all heavenly inhabitants to participate in. With all that we will do in heaven, being able to do it without sin or even the ability to have a bad attitude will be exhilarating. Never again will anyone there ever experience pain, suffering, sorrow, worry, doubt, confusion, frustration, fear, loss, hatred, envy, loneliness, boredom, rejection, apathy, lack of self-control, or anger. You will be perfect and everything, everywhere, and at all times will be perfect. Imagine a life like that! Is this a place you would like to be? Do you know how to get there? Are you going there? Do you know for sure?

Part Four—Section 14

Many times throughout the Bible there is mention of the "Book of Life." The book of Revelation refers to it as the "Lambs Book of Life" *(Revelation 21:27)*. This is an actual book in heaven where the names of every child of God ever born are recorded. There will be no one in heaven whose name has not been written into the Book of Life. Interestingly, the Bible declares that the names were written in this special book before the foundations of the world or people were even created *(Revelation 13:8, 17:8)*. This idea is a bit mind boggling. Remember, God is not bound to the limits of time as we know it. He actually created time for us. As sovereignty and omniscience are part of His holy attributes, God knows and foreknew the names of every person who would ever come to trust Him as Lord. In knowing this, He entered their names, hopefully your name, into the Book of Life prior to creation. In reality, before you were even born God chose you to be a part of His kingdom. Your name was written in His book before your first breath *(Ephesians 1:4)*.

Since God chose you, you are His and He will never lose you no matter what difficulty or doubt you may be facing *(John 6:39)*. Why God chooses some and not others is a mystery the Bible does not explain. Be assured, the Bible clearly states that God has chosen His children in eternity past and refers to them throughout Scripture as "the elect" and "the chosen" of God *(2 Timothy 1:9)*. Though He chose you and is fully responsible for restoring a relationship with you, you have an active role in His plan as your redemption unfolds from your birth to your glorification. What confidence and assurance we can have that we are God's children and no one can snatch us from His grasp, or separate us from His love *(Romans 8:38-39)*.

There are three kinds of people in existence today. There are those who have been saved by Christ and love and serve Him whole heartedly. There are those who have been saved by Christ and are temporarily in a season of confusion, trial, or deception and are having a struggle walking with Christ as they should, or have fallen out of fellowship with the Lord. Then there are those who flat out reject Christ, or have chosen to follow their own plan instead of God's. According to the Bible, you are either a child God and are part of His eternal plans, or you are a child of Satan and will participate in the plans God has for him. You cannot serve two masters. Some of God's children include those whose names have been written in the Book of Life, but have yet to come to an understanding of salvation through Christ. Remember, God knows the beginning from the end. Everyone who comes to terms with Christ does it at different points down life's road at God's appointed time.

If you are a follower of Christ and are currently going through a difficult season in your walk with Him, be assured the Lord will give you strength and will restore the joy of your salvation as you trust Him. In God's love for us, He often has to bring us through times of trial, hardship, or discipline to grow us to the point He wants us to be—especially during times of doubt or rebellion. This process is part of our sanctification where God grows us in holiness to ultimately be more like Christ. As Christians, many times the most substantial moments of spiritual growth and maturity occur at the darkest, most confusing seasons of our lives. Trust God. He is in control and is shaping your life for His glory and eternal purposes.

Part Four—Section 15

You may have many doubts and questions about Jesus Christ, the Bible, or what salvation means. It is a lot to take in. The fact that you are still reading this book and haven't thrown it out the window, stomped on it, or cursed at it is a good sign. The Lord is undoubtedly using this as a tool to minister to you. His purpose is to bring you to a knowledge and understanding of the truth of Jesus Christ and the means of eternal salvation through Christ. This is fully and freely available to you as a gift from God. It is quite possible that your name has even been written in the Book of Life, you just don't know why or what to do next. If that sounds interesting, keep reading!

In understanding salvation through Christ, you have to first have an understanding of what Christ is saving you from. Essentially, God is saving you from yourself! You have a terminal disease that you were born with; only this disease not only kills your body, but your eternal soul. The disease we were born with and have struggled with all our lives is sin. We did not bring this problem on ourselves, but we have sure embraced it.

The nature and desire to sin was passed down to us as a curse, or consequence for mankind rejecting the kindness and provisions of God. Sin has destroyed humanity at its core and humanity's relationship with God. God's first created human, Adam, brought this curse to his offspring when he chose to disobey God's rules *(Romans 5:12-19)*. What Adam did is actually a perfect definition of sin—breaking God's laws. God created man to be in perfect relationship with Him. That relationship was severed by the filth of sin, something God cannot tolerate or commune with since He is absolute holiness and righteousness.

If a doctor were to do an examination on a patient and find out that the patient was going to die from an illness that unless treated would be fatal, and the doctor did nothing to cure the illness or let alone tell the patient they were sick, that doctor would be cruel. The patient would die in ignorance. We have not been left in the dark about this disease we have, or what the cure for this disease is. The Doctor has correctly diagnosed us and informed us of the problem and situation we are in. He tops off His diagnosis with the cure. We can either say: "Doctor, you're crazy. I'm as healthy as I've ever been. Or, Doctor, thank you. I accept your diagnosis and give you permission to treat me and restore my health." What would you say?

God gave man the choice to either receive Him, or reject Him. Man chose to reject Him. The consequence for that rejection is to be eternally separated from God. God could have stopped right there and let mankind grovel in his filth or destroyed us all, but He didn't. As part of God's master plan for humanity He chose to demonstrate to all of His creation, for all of eternity, certain attributes that could never have been displayed unless this happened. Some of those attributes are His unconditional love, forgiveness, grace, mercy, kindness, justice, and the list goes on. In the end, God will receive glory, honor, and praise for revealing Himself to His creation in this way. It is a win-win situation. God gets the glory and man still gets to choose to receive His acceptance of us, or reject it.

Here's what God has done for us to cure our sin disease and to restore us to a relationship with Him. First, He created each of us with His holy laws written on our hearts *(Romans 2:15)*. We all have a conscience and know it is wrong to murder, lie, steal, and so on. In fact, our conscience even tells us there is a God. We can either pursue that God given drive to know Him, or not. Along with that, He gave us the creation. We are without excuse when we can visibly observe the marvelous handiwork of the Creator and either praise Him, or scoff Him in disbelief *(Romans 1:20)*.

God then told us what His laws were in written form. He gave Moses the Ten Commandments written on stone as a material testament that could not be denied of what He wants each of us to do, or not to do *(Exodus 20)*. They are simple enough to be understood by children. Those laws were then passed down from generation to generation and were copied and written in His Holy Word—the Bible for all to see and understand. The Ten Commandments were not given to us by God to mock our dire condition, or to put salt in the wounds of our human inadequacies. The laws were given as a tool used like an x-ray to examine and pinpoint the disease of sin in each of our lives.

It should not take long as we look at our life in the mirror of God's laws to realize that we severely fall short of His perfect, holy, and righteous standards and deserve the justice of His judgment. How many lies have you ever told? Have you ever stolen anything, ever, even as a child? Have you ever wanted something that belonged to someone else? Have you ever taken the Lord's name in vain and used it as a curse word? Have you ever looked at someone with lustful thoughts? Jesus said if you have, you committed adultery in your heart *(Matthew 5:27-28)*. Have you ever been unjustly angry at someone? Jesus said again that if you have, you are a murderer at heart. This is the everyday reality of our condition for everyone on the planet. If you are honestly assessing yourself within God's holy standards you can see you should be in big trouble. And this only covers half of the commandments. If God is just in judging sin, do you think you may need some help?

Throughout history, God has directed the affairs of mankind in remarkable ways that cannot be ignored or denied. In days of old, He spoke His Word directly through the mouths of prophets to warn, teach, and guide the people regarding His ways. He has manifested Himself in physical forms to many chosen people to give messages, warnings, direction, and guidance as evidence that He cares for us and desires deeply that we follow Him and can relate to Him. These wondrous works He has done for us are recorded in a book given to us to read, study, and contemplate. With this we can learn who God is, what He has done for us, and what our future holds for us in Him.

The Bible is God breathed, divinely scripted, and are His words infused through the mind and heart of man. It is in essence, a love letter from God to His people compiled of 66 books, composed by 40 authors, over a time span of about 1500 years. There has and never will be a literary work of art as profound and powerful as this. This book is alive and will endure forever *(Hebrews 4:12)*. The power of God's Word is a tool for building, a weapon for warfare, and food for the soul. Its contents hold the truth to everything we will ever need to know about God and His plans and desires for us in this life *(2 Timothy 3:16-17)*.

To fail to acknowledge and obey the truth of God's Word would be to fail at life. That failure has consequences.

God made it very clear to man in the beginning that the only acceptable offering for sin is the sacrifice of innocent blood. He promised that one day He would send a Savior to solve this sin problem and crush the works of Satan. In the mean time until the Savior came, God established a temporary sacrificial system for sin involving the killing of animals to cover man's sin. This by no means cleansed man from their sin, but only delayed God's judgment until that judgment could be placed upon that final and perfect sacrifice, the Son of God—Jesus Christ. Animal sacrifices were merely a symbolic illustration of what Jesus Christ would accomplish on the cross.

This is ultimately the truest way God has shown His love, mercy, grace, and kindness towards us in that He chose to take the burden of man's sin and place it upon Himself. To defeat death was the reason Christ came to the earth. Jesus Christ willingly left His heavenly throne and clothed Himself in human flesh. Having been miraculously born of a virgin He obtained humanity, yet retained His deity with having a heavenly Father. This allowed Him to be fully human and fully God at the same time. On the earth He declined to display His glory and majesty and humbled Himself to that of a servant. In the flesh He was able to overcome any human desires to sin and lived a blameless, spotless life *(Hebrews 4:15)*. A sinless life paved the way for the ultimate sacrifice that He could now bear. The cost was high, but the price had to be paid for restoration to be complete.

On that fateful yet triumphant day, Christ was murdered. A death sentence applied to an innocent Man is not just, but justice was rendered in the heavenly realm. God the Father looked at His Son and turned His face away. The sin load Christ was bearing was putrid in the eyes of His Father. Christ completed the task He was sent here to do. Jesus at His last breath declared in Aramaic, "Tel Telesti" meaning, "it is finished." All the prophecies up to His death had now been fulfilled and the wage had been paid. He voluntarily gave up His spirit in death relinquishing it to the Father.

After three days in the tomb, the slain body of Christ received new life and the Lord rose from the dead. Without the resurrection, Christ's death would have been meaningless. This was the proof needed to show that sin and death had been defeated and no more was man in bondage to that curse. Christ submitted His sacrifice to God the Father and the payment was received and the debt canceled. Your eternal judgment and penalty for your sin was paid in full by Jesus Christ. On the day you stand before God, He will not see your sin or any of the horrible things you've ever done, but will only see the shed blood of Jesus Christ that covers your soul. Your life has been justified in Christ and you will be found worthy for entrance into God's kingdom.

This gift is something you could never earn. It was given to you by Jesus Christ. His only desire now is that you receive this gift, this pardon that He offers you. Just understand, it is not in your power, ability, nor are you in any position to accept God on your terms. God accepts you based on the merits and sacrifice of Jesus Christ alone! God is fully responsible for saving you! You just simply need to choose to receive His acceptance of you. This decision is available, but will never be forced upon you. How is this gift received?

Part Four—Section 16

Let the truth of the Word of God reveal the way to receive God's acceptance. Here are a few among many of the Bible's most common salvation verses.

Romans 6:23 For the wages of sin is death, but the gift of God is eternal life in Christ Jesus our Lord.

John 14:6 Jesus said to him, "I am the way, the truth, and the life. No one comes to the Father except through Me.

John 11:25-26 25 Jesus said to her, "I am the resurrection and the life. He who believes in Me, though he may die, he shall live. 26 And whoever lives and believes in Me shall never die. Do you believe this?"

I Timothy 2:5-6 5 For there is one God and one Mediator between God and men, the Man Christ Jesus, 6 who gave Himself a ransom for all, to be testified in due time…

Acts 4:12 Nor is there salvation in any other, for there is no other name under heaven given among men by which we must be saved."

John 3:35-36 35 The father loves the Son, and has given all things into His hand. 36 He who believes in the Son has everlasting life; and he who does not believe the Son shall not see life, but the wrath of God abides on him."

John 3:16-17 16 For God so loved the world that He gave His only begotten Son, that whoever believes in Him should not perish but have everlasting life. 17 For God did not send His Son into the world to condemn the world, but that the world through Him might be saved.

1 Peter 3:18 For Christ also suffered once for sins, the just for the unjust, that He might bring us to God, being put to death in the flesh but made alive by the Spirit.

Romans 10:9-10, 13 9 …that if you confess with your mouth the Lord Jesus and believe in your heart that God has raised Him from the dead, you will be saved. 10 For with the heart one believes unto righteousness, and with the mouth confession is made unto salvation. 13 For "whoever calls on the name of the Lord shall be saved."

1 John 1:9 If we confess our sins, He is faithful and just to forgive us our sins and to cleanse us from all unrighteousness.

Mark 1:14-15 14 Now after John was put in prison, Jesus came to Galilee, preaching the gospel of the kingdom of God, 15 and saying, "The time is fulfilled, and the kingdom of God is at hand. Repent, and believe in the gospel."

Romans 1:16 For I am not ashamed of the gospel of Christ, for it is the power of God to salvation for everyone who believes…

Act 3:19 Repent therefore and be converted, that your sins may be blotted out, so that times of refreshing may come from the presence of the Lord,

Luke 5:31-32 31 Jesus answered and said to them, "Those who are well have no need of a physician, but those who are sick. 32 I have not come to call the righteous, but sinners, to repentance."

Acts 17:30-31 30 Truly, these times of ignorance God overlooked, but now commands all men everywhere to repent, 31 because He has appointed a day on which He will judge the world in righteousness by the Man whom He has ordained. He has given assurance of this to all by raising Him from the dead."

2 Corinthians 7:10 For godly sorrow produces repentance leading to salvation, not to be regretted; but the sorrow of the world produces death.

Part Four—Section 17

There are two themes for salvation that seem to pervade the New Testament scriptures—believing in Jesus Christ and repenting of sin. Both are critical for receiving God's acceptance. Both need to be understood correctly. Belief is an action, not a stagnant thought process. Merely having head knowledge of Jesus Christ and what He did is not at all what constitutes "believing." The book of James states that even the demons believe and tremble *(James 2:19)*. Believing is the building block for faith, which is essential to our salvation. The two words can almost be used interchangeably.

If you believe in Jesus Christ, you trust Him. If you trust Him, you love Him. If you love Him, you will obey Him. And by obeying Him, you serve Him. Trusting, loving, obeying, and serving the Lord Jesus Christ is what a believing faith in Him is all about. This will be the evidence of your faith and proof that what you have in Jesus is much more than religion, but a personal and everlasting relationship. This above all else is God's desire for each one of us—that we will partner with Him in His plans and be by His side in a one on one relationship that transcends all human understanding.

The other aspect of believing in Christ is trusting Him with your sin through godly, sorrowful, heartfelt repentance. Just like believing, repentance is an action, not an idea. It is a matter of the heart and will, not just the mind. Simply put, repentance is acknowledging and understanding your sin, knowing that in your sin without Christ you are eternally lost and deserve His condemnation. With that knowledge, you then confess your sin before God and turn from sin. You consciously change directions and with all your heart and soul let God cleanse you from your sin and don't go back to that old life. In this life we will all struggle with sin from time to time, but as a believer in Christ sin no longer has any place controlling your life *(Romans 6:6)*. Repentance and confessing your sin before God is a lifelong pursuit. It is part of our daily walk with the Lord until the day we are glorified in His kingdom when sin will no longer pester our lives.

Through a believing faith in the Lord Jesus Christ and repentance from sin, you can be assured that God has saved you and has accepted you into His kingdom. You are now a child of God—a new creation in Christ Jesus *(2 Corinthians 5:17)*. Your spirit has been re-born *(John3:3)*. You have passed from death into life *(John 5:24)*. You have not earned your way into God's graces, but have received the gift of salvation offered to you by Jesus Christ through faith in Him *(Ephesians 2:8-9)*. Your salvation is a one-time deal. Once you have been saved, you belong to God. He will never let you go.

The Bible declares, *As far as the east is from the west, so far has He removed our transgressions from us (Psalm 103:12)*. All of your sin, past, present, and future, has been wiped clean from your record through the shed blood of Christ on the cross. God will not remember or hold you accountable for your sins on the day you stand before Him. Your sin is gone and you are no longer under condemnation. Thank you Jesus!

Upon receiving salvation through Jesus Christ, what happens next is quite amazing! At the moment of your spiritual re-birth, the Holy Spirit of God baptizes you and comes to dwell within you *(Acts 1:4-8)*. You are united into one giant body of believers in Christ all joined together by the Holy Spirit *(1 Corinthians 12:13)*. God Himself lives inside you. Think about that. You are now a part of the body of Christ and if you allow Him, He will use you mightily for His purposes.

Along with His Spirit, God grants each new believer with spiritual gifts *(1 Corinthians 12:4-11)*. These spiritual giftings are unique to each individual and are graciously given to help the body of Christ and His mission *(Romans 12:3-8)*. God equips you with all the tools necessary to live an abundant, triumphant life for Him *(Ephesians 4:11-16)*. As the process of sanctification begins in your life where God continuously grows you in holiness and righteousness, you may find that your spiritual gifts become more pronounced and alive in your life. You may even discover new gifts you never knew you possessed. Allow God to use you and shape your life into His image and for His purposes. Understand, you are not in control of your destiny, the Lord is, and He has great plans for your future *(Jeremiah 29:11)*.

Part Four—Section 18

As your life begins to transform in Christ, there are many changes and desires you will notice begin to take hold.

1. You will have a hatred for sin and despise the comfortable secret sins you once enjoyed.

2. You will have a desire to learn, read, and share God's Word.

3. You will have a passion for Jesus Christ. He should be precious to you.

4. You will have a desire to be gathered with other believers in fellowship.

5. You will be continually growing in holiness and will become a more mature believer with greater understanding as His Word comes alive in your life.

6. You will notice a sense of joy, fullness, and completeness to your life.

7. You will have a desire to know God personally and will seek Him often in prayer.

8. You will notice the fruits of the Spirit as laid out in *Galatians 5:22* being developed in your life: love, joy, peace, patience, kindness, goodness, faithfulness, gentleness, and self-control.

9. You will have a desire to share the gospel of Christ with the lost.

10. You will earnestly seek and await the return of Christ our Lord.

If you happen to be living in times of trouble and distress, hold fast to your faith in Christ and the Word of God. Keep your eyes open for opportunities to make an eternal impact on someone else's life.

Consider doing for one person what you wish you could do for everyone, and then do it. You have been created for such a time as this. You hold the Words of Life within your heart and soul. Share them with others. You only have one chance in this life to make an eternal impression. Do not waste this opportunity!

Ephesians 2:10 says: *For we are His workmanship, created in Christ Jesus for good works, which God prepared beforehand that we should walk in them. Matthew 6:19-21* encourages us to lay up for ourselves *"treasures in heaven."* Those treasures are our eternal rewards we will receive at the Judgment Seat of Christ for our obedient service to God. Being a doer of the Word of God and not just a hearer of the Word, will be the route to accomplishing the good works the Lord has prepared for you to do (James 1:22-25). Your obedience will secure unimaginable rewards in heaven, given to you by your Heavenly Father for your service to His Son. You will finish the race strong and will be granted the privilege of being an *"overcomer"* as you enter God's heavenly kingdom *(Revelation 2:7).*

Part Four—Section 19

In the last days, the Bible says that deception of the truth and Word of God will be prevalent over the face of the earth. Now is the time more than ever to have a solid, unwavering belief in the biblical foundations our Christian faith is based upon. Here is some scriptural proof as to what will be common in these last days.

> *Galatians 1:8-9 8 But even if we, or an angel from heaven, preach any other gospel to you than what we have preached to you, let him be accursed. 9 As we have said before, so now I say again, if anyone preaches any other gospel to you than what you have received, let him be accursed.*

> *1 Timothy 4:1 Now the Spirit expressly says that in latter times some will depart from the faith, giving heed to deceiving spirits and doctrines of demons...*

> *2 Timothy 4:3-4 3 For the time will come when they will not endure sound doctrine, but according to their own desires, because they have itching ears, they will heap up for themselves teachers; 4 and they will turn their ears away from the truth, and be turned aside to fables.*

Understanding the essentials and being rooted in the gospel of Christ is crucial to assuring you don't fall for the deception of the evil one. There can be disagreements among believers about different interpretations of Scripture as it relates to certain doctrines and minor issues of the faith, but the "essentials" must not be wavered on.

In 325 A.D., the early Church fathers gathered together at the First Council of Nicaea to adopt a statement of faith that could last the generations. This statement would solidify the core tenants of the Christian faith, so that heresy and false teaching could not creep in and delude the foundational principles of the gospel of Christ.

Nicene Creed

(Modern English Version)

We believe in one God, the Father, the Almighty, maker of heaven and earth, of all that is, seen and unseen. We believe in one Lord, Jesus Christ, the only Son of God, eternally begotten of the Father, God from God, light from light, true God from true God, begotten, not made, one in being with the Father. For us and for our salvation He came down from heaven: by the power of the Holy Spirit He was born of the Virgin Mary and became truly human. For our sake He was crucified under Pontius Pilate; He suffered, died and was buried. On the third day He rose again in fulfillment of the Scriptures; He ascended into heaven and is seated at the right hand of the Father. He will come again in glory to judge the living and the dead, and His kingdom will have no end. We believe in the Holy Spirit, the Lord, the giver of life, who proceeds from the Father and the Son, who with the Father and the Son is worshipped and glorified, who has spoken through the prophets. We believe in one holy catholic and apostolic Church. We acknowledge one baptism for the forgiveness of sins. We look for the resurrection of the dead, and the life of the world to come. Amen.

As you live out your days, make prayer a pattern for your life *(Philippians 4:6-7)*. Prayer has the power to shut up the flood gates of hell and open the windows of heaven. God hears and responds to the prayers of a righteous man or woman of God *(James 5:16)*. Take all opportunities to gather with and befriend fellow believers in Christ. They are your brothers and sisters and a gift from the Lord in providing fellowship, strength, encouragement, and accountability during troubling times *(Hebrews 10:25)*.

Lastly, let the words of the Apostle Paul motivate you as you move forward in your walk with the Lord. *But you be watchful in all things, endure afflictions, do the work of an evangelist, fulfill your ministry (2 Timothy 4:5)*.

May the Heavenly Father bless and guide you by the truth of the Word of God and direction of the Holy Spirit as you embrace an eternal relationship with your God and Savior—Jesus Christ. Amen.

Appendix

Systematic Prayer Guide

Praying, how you pray, and how often you pray is one of the most important and crucial aspects to the life of a follower of Jesus Christ. Praying can be difficult and at times may even seem impossible to do. Lack of focus, concentration, motivation, and desire are all issues that every believer struggles with from time to time when it comes to prayer. One way to overcome this would be to pray to God for help with praying. This may seem redundant, but who is a better guide to help you speak to God than God Himself through the direction and comfort of the Holy Spirit. May this prayer guide be a blessing for your life and possibly an answer to prayer in helping you draw closer to your Heavenly Father through prayer.

Pray For: P.L.A.C.E.S.

People **L**ocations **A**ssistance **C**hurch **E**ternal Focus **S**alvation

- **Monday—People:** Pray for your immediate family, spouse, children, parents, etc… Be creative as to what to pray about for those closest in your life. You know them better than anyone, so finding things to pray about should not be a problem.

- **Tuesday—People:** Pray for your extended family, friends, and acquaintances. People is a big category, so breaking them down into groups on different days should make it easier to get everyone and their needs in.

- **Wednesday—Locations:** Wednesday is an opportunity to pray for missionaries in locations around the world, as well as the persecuted church and believers who live in places unfriendly to the gospel. You can also pray for your city, state, country, bad neighborhoods, neighboring churches, or areas that seem to be heavy demonic strongholds.

- **Thursday—Assistance:** We can't walk this walk on our own. God's assistance and direction is at times all we have to hold on to as we pursue the plans He has for us. Take time to pray for the areas of your life you are struggling in, or need help with. Let God help you get your walk right with Him. If you are struggling, this can negatively affect all areas of your life and others. When you're soaring with the Lord everything else you do will be positively affected.

- **Friday—Church:** Pray for your local church service on Sunday morning or other services throughout the week, evening services, bible studies, prayer groups etc... Pray for all areas of the service including those who attend, Sunday school, worship, prayer time, fellowship, and the sermon. This is also a good time to pray specifically for your pastors and church leadership. Pray also for other local churches in your area, and the Church of Christ abroad.

- **Saturday—Eternal Focus:** Having an eternally biblical world view and mindset will change the way you think and act in all areas of your life. Pray that you are constantly thinking about and on the watch for opportunities the Lord provides, where you can make an impact that will last for eternity. Pray for these opportunities to arise. Pray also for boldness to be obedient to God when these eternal opportunities do come your way. Whether it is speaking words of encouragement to someone going through a difficult time or sharing the gospel with an unbeliever, God will use you to change other people's lives forever. This process will change your own life. If you are watching and obedient, the seeds you can plant on fertile soil are endless.

- **Sunday—Salvation:** Use this time to pray for the salvation of anyone the Lord puts on your mind; unsaved family, friends, co-workers, acquaintances, neighbors, the list goes on. Over the course of the previous week you undoubtedly came across scores of people you either saw, or had conversations with that you know do not have a right relationship with God. Many of these people will stick in your mind. Pray for their salvation. It does not take long and could be the final prayer the Lord uses to kindle the fire in their soul that will burn for Him for eternity.

This prayer guide is just that, a guide. Use it as it is, tweak it, alter it any way you feel led. The idea is structured, sound, and easy to follow and adjust. As time goes on it will be automatic. You will know exactly when to pray and what to pray for. If you skip a day, don't worry about it. This is not meant to be perfect. Prayer is not perfect, it doesn't have to be. Just pick back up on whatever day of the week it is and move forward. Be assured, God will honor your faithfulness and diligence as you align your will with that of the Father's.

Consider one more idea regarding how much time you should spend alone with the Lord daily, either in prayer, reading the Word, or personal devotions. Think about how much time the average person has in a day. Most people sleep eight hours, work eight hours, and have about eight hours to do with as they please. Time is the one thing besides our money that the Lord has given us discretion on how we spend it. A wise Christian has already learned the value of tithing their money, or gladly giving a portion of their income to the work of the Lord through the church. A tithe, or ten percent, is always a good place to start when it comes to giving.

How about tithing your time? You probably have eight hours a day, some more or less, that you use in various ways. Eight hours is 480 minutes, so a tithe of that time would be 48 minutes per day. If that seems like an unreasonable amount of time to give God, then re-examine the priorities in your life. Maybe you need to weed out some idols. You may have to break it down into two time periods that add up to that amount. Do it. In that amount of time, what you can accomplish and the growth you can achieve in the Lord will be staggering. Just as the Lord blesses you for your faithful giving of money, imagine the blessings He will pour out on your life for giving a portion of your life—your time back to Him. It's all His anyway. Just think about that.

ORDER FORM

✉ **Email orders:**
cloudboundpublishers@gmail.com

📄 **Mail orders:**
Cloudbound Publishers
P.O. Box 1350
Astoria, OR 97103

$12.00 includes shipping & handling

$10.00 includes shipping & handling

Purchase a PDF of this book on a USB flash drive—Plug into your computer and read, email, or print at your convenience.

✂---

Please send me the following items:

TITLE	QUANTITY	PRICE
The Rapture, the Remnant, and the Return (softcover)		
Wooden cross pendant flash drive (Flash-Book)		
Make checks payable to Cloudbound Publishers **TOTAL**		

(Additional discounts for bulk orders are available.)

Name: _____

Address: _____

City: _____ State: _____ Zip: _____

Telephone: _____ Email: _____

Card number: _____ CVC: _____

Name on the card: _____ Exp. date: _____

Credit cards processed with PayPal

Books also available from Amazon.com
Ebooks available from Amazon and Barnes & Noble